Speaking Faith:
The Essential Handbook for Religion Communicators

Editor: J. Richard Peck
Designer: Bret D. Haines
Cover and section page designs: UMR Communications
Executive Producers: Jeanean D. Merkel and Shirley Whipple Struchen

7th Edition

Printed with support from the National Council of Churches USA, an association of 36 national faith groups with programs in communication, media advocacy, and commitment to interfaith relations. www.ncccusa.org

With special thanks for concept to Barry Creech, Dick Duerksen, Frederick Gonnerman, Ava Martin, Kimberly Pace, Wesley "Pat" Pattillo, and David Porter and for production assistance to Kay Fielder and Mandy Vasquez of UMR Communications.

As the Religion Communicators Council celebrates its 75th anniversary, we're proud to present this latest edition of our how-to handbook, first published 35 years ago.

1969	1st edition	Jim Suggs
1976	2nd edition	W. C. Fields
1982	3rd edition	Charles DeVries
1988	4th edition	Jim Steele
1995	5th edition	Tom Slack
2000	6th edition	Linda Post Bushkofsky
2004	7th edition	J. Richard Peck

ISBN No. 0-9679757-1-9

Table of Contents

Introduction by Diana Eck i

I. Communication: What's All the Fuss?

Chapter 1—Discover Your Mission 3

By Kimberly Pace

Chapter 2—The Communicator Is a Person, Not a Phone 11

By M. Garlinda Burton

II. "If I Had a Hammer:" The Tools of Communicating

Chapter 3—Getting Out The News: Communicating With Secular Journalists 21

By Brad Pokorny

Chapter 4—Graphic Identity: Do You Know Who You Are? Do They? 27

By Nancy Fisher and Jay Sidebotham

Chapter 5—Get the Picture? 33

By Bret Haines

Chapter 6—Design: Do It Yourself Demo 39

By Kami Lund and Linda Svensk

Chapter 7—Hiring a Communications Consultant 45

By J. Ron Byler

Chapter 8—Media: Didn't I See You on TV? 51

By Kermit Netteburg

Chapter 9—Surfing Your Faith Community:
Building a Presence on The World Wide Web 59

By Jeanean D. Merkel

Chapter 10—Electronic Presentations: Not the Same Old Song and Dance 69

By Rose Pacatte, F.S.P.

Chapter 11—Other Electronic Tools of Communication 75

By Bill Southern

Chapter 12—Strategic Communication:

Promoting Your Faith Community in Good Faith 83

By Donn James Tilson

III. "We've Got the Whole World in Our Hands:"
Communicating in the Larger Community

Chapter 13—We've Got a Situation Here: Crisis Communication 115

By Daniel R. Gangler

Chapter 14—America Is Interfaith 123

By Anuttama Dasa

Chapter 15—A Crash Course in Copyrights:

Ethical Issues Related to Communications 133

By Rachel Riensche

Chapter 16—What's Beyond? The Communication Future 141

By Gary R. Rowe

Authors 151

Communicating Religion: Challenges for the New Millennium
An Introductory Word

Diana L. Eck

Communicating religion in the twenty-first century is no easy matter. Religion is fast-changing and so are the means and speed of communication. In one sense, the time and space dimensions of our world have collapsed. We can send instant messages via electronic mail to colleagues, friends, and family on the other side of the world. On the World Wide Web and through satellite telecommunications, we can have instant access to images and news releases from around the world. From my study in Cambridge, Massachusetts, I can read the *Times* of India from New Delhi or the *Bozeman Daily Chronicle* from my hometown in Montana. And yet the "we" is all the while becoming more complex and in many ways more fragmented. Some of us in the human community participate in this new time-space world; others still live many hours from the nearest telephone. Some of us have access to communication budgets and strategies that can shape the image of religious communities, peoples, and nations. Others do not. Even as the world is knit together by the fibers of communications, we are more aware than ever of the chasms of cultural and religious difference, stereotypes, misleading images, and outright enmity that separate us.

Along with the globalization of world systems, the 21st century has brought a new and more complex demographic reality. The movement of people as refugees and as economic and political migrants has created a new cultural and religious landscape in many parts of the world, including the United States. In the past 40 years, people have come to the U.S. from all over the world, bringing with them not only their dreams of freedom and economic success, but also their religious traditions. One of the hallmarks of our era is the marbling of the world's religions in America. There are mosques and Islamic communities across the country from Portland, Maine to San Diego, California. Hindu, Jain, and Buddhist temples are visible new additions to the religious landscape of cities and towns all across America. Not only have distant neighbors become close through powerful means of communications, once-distant neighbors are now next-door neighbors because of the new immigration.

The challenge of communicating across cultures and religious traditions, now just across the street, is a new one for many American faith communities. It requires careful listening and learning. All over America, especially in the past decade, new forms of interfaith dialogue are emerging—including hundreds of interfaith councils and partnerships. These are new instruments of relationship, bringing people together in intentional and often very creative ways. Some interfaith groups have limited their circle of communication to Jews, Christians, and Muslims, the so-called Abrahamic faiths. But in communicating this new interfaith reality, we all must be careful to recognize the built-in exclusions when Buddhist, Sikh, or Hindu neighbors are elided from mention and image.

Interfaith dialogue and communication has enormous educational importance. Most people in the majority Christian religious communities of America have too little knowledge of Muslims, Sikhs, or Hindus. And some of what we do know is shaped by stereotype and half-truth. Bear in mind, however, many of our new neighbors have relatively little understanding of Christian and Jewish communities too, and that may also be shaped by stereotype and fragmentary experience. Communication is a two-way street. It offers everyone the opportunity to know and be known.

One of the great gifts of the communications revolution is that each religious community can represent itself—in image, voice, and word. For some communities, this means that after centuries of relying on the interpretations and misinterpretations of others, they can define themselves in their own terms. The Jamaat-I-Islami in India and Pakistan packages its Islamic views for the English language Internet. So does the world Hindu organization called the Vishva Hindu Parishad and the Taiwan-based Fo-Kuang Movement of Buddhist Humanism. So does the World Council of Churches, the Southern Baptist Convention and the United Church of Christ. The World Wide Web provides the unprecedented opportunity to present ourselves as we would like to be known and to receive the self-presentation of others. It reminds us, however, that even when our primary audience is our own religious community, we are always overheard by our neighbors, and we must communicate in full consciousness of this reality.

Given our new global and local situation, the communication of religion is more important than ever before. The Religion Communicators Council has put serious thought into the critical task of communicating religion through the powerful and varied forms of media—word and image, radio, television, and the World Wide Web. Religion is both a deeply personal and powerfully public matter. Both the deep intimacy and the highly charged electricity of religion make the task of communication difficult. At the personal level, matters of faith and heart are subtle and complex, and effective communication often requires sound-bite simplicity. We must never forget, however, that the bearers of our religious traditions are people—not systems and abstractions, ideologies and creeds. As for the public dimensions of religion, we know all too well how religious language, symbol, and image can readily become the symbolic fuel for powerful political and social movements. In the fires of public discussion, terms like "ten commandments," "jihad," and "head-scarf" may be swept into a kind of shorthand in which all perspective and rational analysis is lost.

In the United States, communicating about religion requires yet another kind of vigilance: distinguishing between a religious and a civic voice. All of us who are part of a religious tradition often speak and write out of the sources and perspectives of our own religious faith, and when we do so publicly, it is important to indicate that point of view. "Speaking as a Christian, I would say. . ." But we are also citizens, and as such we speak and write out of the sources and perspectives of our common constitutional covenants as citizens. "As a citizen, however, I would insist. . . ." Here we need to develop the bridging language that enables us to communicate effectively in a public context. This is the common speech of the civic arena and it should not be laden with the presumed religious language of the majority. Our constitutional democracy deliberately has created space for people of all religious traditions—and none. We may switch lanes between our religious and civic voices, but when we do so, it is important to use turn signals.

These are critical and exciting times. Never have the means of communication been easier and more expansive. And never has communicating religion been more challenging or important.

Dr. Diana Eck is a professor of comparative religion at Harvard University. She has been involved in the Pluralism Project (www.pluralism.org), an ongoing study of religious diversity in the United States, and is the author of many books, including *A New Religious America: How a "Christian Country" Has Become the World's Most Religiously Diverse Nation* and *On Common Ground: World Religions in America*.

I. Communication:

What's All the Fuss?

Chapter 1

Discover Your Mission

By Kimberly Pace

Why is it important to discover the mission of your faith group?

Your mission should be that which drives all the work you do. If the mission statement is inadequate or unclear, it will be difficult to properly focus your communication vehicles. Many times faith groups spend days creating a mission statement that, in the end, does not really meet their needs. An effective mission statement must reflect the unique gifts of the faith group—who is to be served and what needs are to be met.

The mission statement should succinctly state the purpose, value and meaning of the faith community. A concise and memorable statement will provide a slogan that members can use to explain the purpose of your faith community. It is also the touchstone from which all communications strategy should be modeled. Communicators will finally use the mission statement to evaluate every piece of communication.

 To prepare a mission statement, begin with the following:

Core competency
List all the skills/talents of those in the faith community. Then ask what people in your faith community are really interested in or passionate about. It should be a clear, honest look at your community. You might discover that talents and interests of members are working with children, providing small group settings for older adults, or reaching out to the homeless your area.

Served market
Research where you live and the needs of those who live in community. Is there an arena that no one is serving? This assessment of needs helps you understand your market.

Brand promise
Answer the following questions:

- What unique experience does your faith community offer to your market?
- What unique service can your faith community offer?
- Where is the creator leading you?

Answers to these questions will help you identify your brand. The brand is something that your faith community is never willing to negotiate or compromise. It is what you say about your community when others ask who you are and what you do. It is how you meet the needs of your market.

After discovering your core competency, your market and your brand, you can clearly state your mission. The mission is the basis for all future communications with your faith community, the area in which you live, and the world.

Identify Communication Needs

Why is it important to identify communication needs?

It is all too easy for you to focus on the loudest or the most active audiences you serve. It is also easy to just assume you know the needs of your audiences. You find yourselves using the same communication tools over and over again without really asking whether they are the best way to meet these needs. The truth is that when you identify needs of someone else, you are giving your "best guess" to what their needs are. If you are married, think about your spouse. How many times have you thought you knew what he or she wanted, but really didn't have it right at all? It is the same in identifying the needs of other people and how they prefer to receive communications. To find out, you must ask. You must research.

 The following process can be used by a small group—either a communications team or faith group leadership team—to identify the needs of your audience and to match communication tools.

Step 1 Target Market

List all those in your faith community.
For example, staff, volunteers who lead committees/teams, active members, inactive members, teenagers, children, older adults, etc.

Work in small groups and list the needs under each of those you listed above.
It's important that you put yourselves in their shoes. Think from their perspective and make your best guess.

Decide on the top two needs for each group.
You can't meet all the needs of everyone; focus on the top two.

Step 2 Media Alternatives

Make a list of all the electronic ways in which your faith community does and could communicate with others.
For example, Web site, e-mail, chat rooms, videotapes, CD-Rom, television, radio, fax, etc.

Make a list of all the non-electronic ways in which your faith community does and could communicate with others.
For example, bulletins, newsletters, flyers, posters, door hangers, signs, billboards, letters, etc.

Make a list of all the personal ways in which your faith community does and could communicate with others.
For example, home visits, phone calls, talking with others at work, inviting persons face-to-face, etc.

Step 3 Media Mix

List the communications tools from Media Alternatives that best match the two needs for the groups identified in Target Market.
It is important to have a mix of communication tools from the faith community to reach different people and to meet different needs.

Step 4 Research

Research before you act.

Realize this is only your best guess and you must check to see if you are correct.

This four-step process will help you hear what the team thinks the needs are. These are your hypotheses, your best guesses. Now you are ready to research, discover, and compare the actual needs, and choose the media mix that has the best chance of succeeding.

Establish a Strategic Communications Plan

Why is it important to have a strategic communications plan?

Strategic planning helps you focus communication on initiatives that will have the greatest impact on the mission of your faith group. It enables your group to focus on specific priorities and not try to be everything for everybody. A well-developed plan provides steps that you can follow and helps your community be good stewards of limited resources.

A strategic communications plan should include the following four-step process:

1. Get organized.

Create an organization task chart. What is the current way that you carry out your ministry/work? Who does what for whom?

State the mission of the organization. Core competencies? Served markets/needs? Unique brand promise? Is the mission the same as it has always been, different or in the process of changing?

Form a strategic communications planning team. Who should help us plan? What skills/gifts can they contribute?

Agree on the communications mission. How will you use communications in the current planning period to advance the organizational mission? This is the "job" description for the strategic communications team.

2. Assess current reality.

Look at your environment. What's happening in your neighborhood, town, city, and world? What trends suggest changes need to be made?

List your ministry/work areas. What are your current programs, ministry areas and/or activities? How are they evaluated? What difference do they make?

Do a SWOT analysis. What are the (internal) strengths and weaknesses of your local faith community? What are the (external) opportunities and threats?

3. Set a vision for the future.

Create a desired reality. What do you want your future look like? How is it different from (or better than) what you are currently doing? What is compelling about this vision?

Design your strategy. What should you continue doing that you are doing well and how can you improve upon these activities? What are you not doing that you need to start doing? What do you need to stop doing?

Write communications initiatives. List three to eight things you can do to move from what you are doing now (current reality) to where you want to be in the future (desired reality)?

4. Develop specific action plan(s) for each initiative.

Select the target audience. You will have at least one action plan for each initiative and each initiative will have one or more target audiences. Audiences may be external (prospective members, local community) or internal (current members, staff)

Design the message and media mix. What will be the unique selling proposition for each action plan? How will you deliver these messages?

Assign tasks and objectives. How will each initiative be implemented? By whom? By when? With what result?

Compose a budget. What resources and budget will be needed?

Create evaluation tools. Every action plan needs simple, built-in evaluation tools to monitor what has been accomplished.

Implement a Communications Audit

Why is it important to implement a communications audit?

Most of the time, you spend your energy offering one-way communication—through preaching, leading a small group study, or offering advice. How much time do you spend listening and retrieving information? A communications audit conducted every two to three years offers a practical way to look in depth at how you communicate with other people (internally or externally) and how they communicate back to you. A communications audit can also serve as a benchmark. After a set period of time, launch another communications audit to evaluate what has changed.

A communications audit should include the following:

1. Establish goals and objectives

Identify what it is you want to learn. Are you launching a new program in your faith community and want to know how it will work? Do you want the involvement of people outside your faith community? Do you want to know what people are thinking on a specific subject? Whatever the reason, list the goals and objectives clearly.

Example:
Goal:
Your community wants to know how to reach more people in the neighborhood.

Objectives:

To discover needs of those who live in your neighborhood.

To find out what kinds of communication vehicles raise interest or increase interest.

To evaluate methods and means of sending invitations.

To evaluate all print and electronic pieces sent to potential members.

2. Interview key leaders

Once you've decided on your goals and objectives, compose questions for influence leaders who are members of your community that need to be supportive of a communications audit. You need their enthusiasm to involve others and need their influence to support and implement final recommendations. Interviews with key leaders will help you develop questions for focus groups.

Example:

"What are some of effective ways our faith community reaches out to our neighborhood?"

"What are the needs of those who live in our neighborhood?"

"How can our faith community do a better job in reaching these people?"

3. Establish focus groups

Establish at least five focus groups with 8 to 15 members selected in accordance with your goal and objectives. Members should be chosen at random, but sometimes political considerations may result in establishing more focus groups so everyone feels they have been "heard" and "included" The person facilitating the focus group should be someone highly trusted by all or someone from outside the immediate faith community that can listen objectively. The focus group should have a set time limit. Everyone's opinion and insights matter and the facilitator's role is to guide the process, help everyone stay on the subject, and respect one another. The purpose of the focus group is to gather in-depth perceptions and understanding as they relate to your goal and objectives. Expect to hear things your intuition has already told you, but listen for new information. Most importantly, it's not what you hear in one focus group, but the common themes and trends that you hear through all the focus groups.

Example: Set up five focus groups of persons over age 15 randomly chosen from your neighborhood.

Invite 15 people to each focus group. These should be persons who actually live in the neighborhood, faith-community leaders who work in the neighborhood, some randomly selected faith-community members who have an interest in the neighborhood, neighborhood business owners, chamber of commerce representatives, and neighborhood schoolteachers.

Set the meeting in a common location.

Choose a facilitator to lead all focus groups.

Ask questions, such as,

"What are the greatest needs of those living in your neighborhood?"

"What are some good things that you observe or hear that are helping reach people in your neighborhood?"

"What are some things that your faith community could do to meet some of the needs you expressed?"

"What kinds of communication vehicles do people in your neighborhood, prefer? E-mail? Letters? Face-to-face conversation?

4. Conduct surveys

Send out surveys to a random sampling of persons from whom you are seeking information. The surveys should include a self-stamped return envelope. Surveys might also be posted on a Web site with e-mails and postcards sent to persons to invite them to go on-line to fill out the survey. Most importantly, the survey should give persons the freedom to anonymously express their thoughts and insights.

Example: Mail the surveys to 1,000 randomly selected individuals in the zip code in which your faith community is located.

Ask questions, such as,

> "What do you think is the greatest need in your community?"

> "What are your ideas of what could help?"

> "What do you think your faith community should be doing to help meet these needs?"

"Do you attend worship services in another faith community?"

"If not, what would your faith community need to offer and do in order for you to visit?"

Adapt the survey for members of your faith community.

5. Report findings

Invite professional communicators to analyze your faith community. Have them take a close look at signage, attend a worship service, look at your print pieces, check your Web site, and reflect on your members' attitude, dress, and demeanor. Ask them to evaluate survey results and data from focus group with an eye that which is said over and over. Go for the facts and report findings to everyone in the faith community.

Example: In your survey, you found out that 3 percent of those that responded shared a need for parenting skills and 75 percent said they needed childcare. Even if your faith community has great small groups for parents, there is still a need for daycare.

6. Establish recommendations and a time table.

Now that you have all this information, what are you going to do? Your faith community has taken a risk by asking about needs because people now have the expectation that you will respond in some manner. You don't have to respond to everything, but you must do something. Create recommendations in direct response to the facts and set a timeline for completing them. Do something within the first three months and then a set up a 6-month, 12-month and 18-month plan.

Example: In light of what you've learned, you set up a cleaning day for your faith community. You cut grass, plant flowers, fix the sign, and add safe swing sets and sand box in a children's play area. You put door hangers on homes in your neighborhood, send postcards, put up posters in area businesses and post on your Web site an invitation to parents to attend a "children's neighborhood picnic."

Evaluate Activities

Why is it important to evaluate plans and programs?

With many faith groups, evaluation comes only at the end of the event, program, or publication piece. It is important to think about evaluation as a total communications process. Without evaluation you keep doing the same things while expecting different results. Evaluation helps you understand that present actions do not work. Just because you've invested time in the strategic plan doesn't mean it will work. If an activity doesn't achieve the results you want, evaluate why it didn't work and what you can learn from it. If the evaluation is positive, don't get into a rut. Just because the plan or program has a positive evaluation this year, it may change next year. With every good plan, comes good, consistent evaluation.

Evaluate with A.I.D.A.

Attention

The communication piece must grab people's attention. How will you do this to reach the most people who might be interested in the event, program, resource, or ministry?

Example: You are trying to reach 10 new families with children to come to your annual picnic. You mail out 100 invitations to new families in your neighborhood, post the information on your Web site, put it in the weekly newsletter, and announce it during the worship service. Attention is measured by change in awareness and knowledge of the product or event being communicated.

Interest

How many of the group to which you sent special invitations are actually interested? This is an indication of the "pulling power" or ability of the communication to attract and engage the audience. Is it relevant? Do they pay attention and follow up?

Example: Out of the 100 invitations mailed you have had 30 phone calls or e-mails requesting additional information about the picnic.

Desire

Why would a person want to participate in this event, program, resource, or ministry? This is a measure of the intention to try it out.

Example: Out of the 30 phone calls regarding the picnic you discover that persons searching for a faith community want to know about your child care. They indicate their intention to actually attend.

Action

What does the audience actually do? What is the action you want them to take in response to your communication? How many actually come and/or bring someone else with them? Do they really follow through on their intention?

Example: Fifteen new families attend the picnic. You greet them and ask them why they were interested and why they decided to come. You track this information and put it into your evaluation process. You met your goals of 10 families. Why did you have an extra five? Through asking why they came, you learned that five families came because a member of the faith community personally invited them. They never saw the invitation, but received the information through a third party. This pass-along effect is a "bonus" from the impact of the message on the interest, desire and action of an unexpected audience.

The AIDA process helps communicators set objectives for communication action plans. If you want 10 families to attend (action), you may need 20 who intended to come (desire), 40 who read and saved the announcement (interest), and 80 who saw the announcement or heard about it from some else (awareness). It also helps explain why an action plan succeeds or fail. Evaluation using the AIDA model helps the communicator understand the strengths and weaknesses of the action plan. Low awareness may indicate a failure of the media mix to reach the target audience, while low interest or desire is probably a message problem.

It is important to consider the entire communications process when doing an evaluation. This process typically starts with asking whether anyone even heard the message (awareness) all the way to whether any action resulted (behavior change). A communication plan that gets awareness but fails to stimulate some action is probably not successful.

———————————

Want to go more in-depth with communications strategy and brand awareness?
Check out these books:

Good to Great by Jim Collins

Building the Brand-Driven Business by Scott M. David and Michael Dunn

Value-Added Public Relations by Thomas L. Harris

Basic Communication Resource? Check out *crt.umc.org/guidebook*

Chapter 2

The Communicator is a Person, Not a Phone

By M. Garlinda Burton

A few years ago, when our communications agency decided to purchase a centralized telephone service equipped with voicemail for each of our 100 staff members, I voiced strong opposition.

I'm not one who is opposed to emerging technology; in fact, I rarely leave home without my cell phone, my Pocket PC, my laptop computer, and my portable hard drive. And I use my home answering machine to screen unwanted calls.

Further, I have no quarrel, in general, with voicemail. It is handy for getting messages through in a timely manner and for leaving routine information that would otherwise be unnecessarily delayed or forgotten. I often use voicemail as an audio "to do" list, leaving messages for myself at home or at the office to remind myself of errands or projects that would otherwise slip my mind during my commute.

Still, I was adamant in opposing our voicemail-centered phone system at our agency because it violated my number one principle as a professional communicator and a customer-focused worker: A customer/client deserves timely (dare I say, immediate) personal attention, without having to jump through hoops to get it. The telephone, in my estimation, is first and foremost, a vehicle for getting through to a person who has the information a client wants. It should not be seen or used as a substitute for personal contact, nor should it be the center around which a communications office should be established. Telephones are great tools. But they are not in themselves communicators. Why? Because, at its best, communications implies a two-way exchange; without the potential of a live person on each end of the wire, a telephone can actually thwart, rather than enable communications.

Communications: Caring, accessibility, tailored, and feedback-friendly

At our best, communicators are those who receive and deliver timely, accurate, inspiring, useful—and potentially life-changing—information to a specific person or group of people. Ideally, a faith-based communicator helps to interpret, explain, unearth and make wonderfully clear concepts, ideas, traditions, practices, beliefs, rituals, structures, history and people.

Effective communications starts with a competent, caring, knowledgeable provider of information whose goal is to offer helpful resources in ways that are accessible and tailored for the recipient on the other end. Further, the effective communicator is constantly on the lookout for new information, new means of delivering resources and information and getting feedback from the consumer to increase the value of one's resources to the consumer and strengthen the communication functions. Let's look at these attributes or concepts—caring, accessibility, tailored, and feedback—in light of a telephone system, for example.

Caring: This concept may seem at bit "squishy" in a discussion about professional behavior. However, the most successful advertising firms on Madison Avenue will tell you that building a trusting relationship with consumers—and getting them to feel good about a product or services—is paramount to success. The flip side: demonstrating indifference to or disregard for consumer wants and needs will eventually put you out of business.

Back to our company telephone system: We envisioned voicemail as a way to reduce customer frustration by letting them leave messages instead of staying on hold forever, or listening to a ringing phone and wondering if anyone ever actually comes to work in your shop. A bonus of voicemail was that workers who have to be away from their desks didn't have to miss important calls, could use messages to set priorities about who to call first and could forward messages to the most appropriate persons, rather than requiring callers to dial several numbers before getting the right person to assist them. And if a caller missed her intended party, she could (during stated business hours) dial "0" and get a live person at any time.

Telephone dos and don'ts for communicators and their staff

Change your answering machine daily, or at least if you're away from your phone for an extended period of time.

In your voicemail greeting inform client about any extended absences, let them know when you will be in your office and give them an alternate person to call, based on their needs.

Make your greeting/voicemail message brief, but detailed enough to guide the caller.

Some people refuse to leave voicemail, message because they aren't sure when or if you will check the message. A detailed message will help them decide whether it's worth leaving you a message or when they are more likely to get you in person.

Never put callers on hold.

If you absolutely must put callers on hold, let them know why you're putting them hold, give them an estimate of how long they must hold and offer them an alternative to holding.

> **Wrong:** "Jewish Family Center, please hold." (click)(annoying music plays for three minutes) "Hello, who are you holding for? He's not in; may I ask why you're calling? Please hold." (click)(three more minutes)

> **Right:** "Jewish Family Center. May I help you? I have another call coming in that I must answer. May I put you on hold for a minute or would you like someone to call you back? Yes, if you call back in an hour the other receptionist will be back and we'll be less swamped. Thank you."

Offer to take a number and have a colleague call a client back, even if it's not your job.

When I was editor of *Interpreter*, readers calling about subscription problems were often routed to me by mistake. Rather than risk losing a customer because I blew them off or consigned them to a long wait in our customer service queue, I simply took a minute to take their change-of-address information or took a number and let our Customer Service Team call them back on our dime. That little bit of time and good will bought us lots of loyal and satisfied customers.

That's the way the system is supposed to operate in a workplace where the communications' function is well considered and customer-focused. Is that the way it is in your workplace? Are customers fairly certain that they get voicemail only when necessary? Have all employees been trained on telephone etiquette, so that they leave a short, helpful message for callers and return calls promptly? Do employees have "office hours," when they are usually at their desks and available to answer and return calls? Is there a clearly defined way for callers to get out of "voicemail hell" and getting a real person? Do bosses call into the office occasionally and check the system to ensure calls are answered promptly, customers are treated competently and respectfully, and that the central voice mailbox is functioning properly?

During a break from writing this article, I tried to leave a message during business hours at a local carpet-cleaning company and got a message that the voice mailbox was full. I couldn't get anyone by dialing "0." This was the third day I couldn't get through, so I called another company. A live person answered my query promptly and got my $500 emergency job and a new customer.

Caring communications is demonstrated in several ways, most of them neither costly nor time-consuming. For your telephone system: Make sure that office hours are clearly stated and that your out-of-office voicemail line is staffed during office hours; stagger lunch hours so that phones are staffed during callers' likely calling time; consider phone etiquette training for your entire staff or volunteer team.

In general: if you promise to mail, fax, call or e-mail information to a customer, tell then when you're sending the copy and keep that promise; voice concern and gratitude for customers (i.e., "Thank you so much for calling." "I'm sorry you're having trouble getting that information.").

Accessibility, for a communicator, should be a natural extension of caring. It's simple: Folks have to get to your information and services in order to use them. It's not communications if there is a breakdown between the communicator and the recipient. Merely putting resources "out there" is not enough.

We live in a marvelous time. Never before have there been so many avenues for sending, receiving, storing or retrieving all types of information. Consider e-mail and the Internet. Last night, in about four hours, I put together the 12-page, bimonthly newsletter for my church, using international news, photos, original clip art, and statistical materials, all sent to me and received electronically. I completed the layout and design without touching a sheet of paper, a pair of scissors, or a wooden ruler. However, in order for me to get the materials I needed, the Web sites I searched first had to organize and present their resources in ways that I—an admittedly above-average (but by no means "expert") Web-prowler—could navigate. "Flash" and "Java" are entertaining, but what separates the sites I find useful from the ones I find merely "interesting" are accessibility and ease of use. The best communicators are not necessarily those who know and use the very latest whistles and bells; rather, superlative communicators are those who keep pace with emerging technology, while keeping a finger on the pulse of audience needs. A strong communications program includes ample room for growth as technical need and know-how grows, but also keeps an eye and ear open for what your core audience is requesting and using.

Take my church, for instance. As volunteer communications chairperson (and a professional communicator), I have the tools, money and know-how to put everything we need on the Internet. I've worked in a multimedia company for 20 years, and know about making videos, setting up a multi-line phone system and doing a major marketing campaign. A church newsletter as the central and only regular communications tool, in fact, is a rather prosaic, antiquated way to communicate, according to the circles in which I move.

At my 100-member local church, however, my expertise and technical capabilities must be measured against the resources and needs of our current—and even our potential congregation. About 60 percent of the people who attend my church are homeless or in precarious living situations, and therefore do not own computers or have access to the Internet. Some do spend time in job-readiness, rehabilitation or community centers, where they can surf the 'net and check e-mail. Many of those places get donated computers, usually not the latest models, so they often don't have the capacity to run the most current programs. Our communication budget is extremely limited.

So what we have is a pretty good newsletter, which is mailed to members and friends with addresses, and a new, simplistic Web site with basic information, late-breaking news and event announcements and e-mail links to the pastor, outreach team and the chair of the communication committee. It's a little lowbrow to some, but it works. And those who need or want information about and access to our church can get it.

 To determine how accessible your communication resources are to your intended customers and audiences, ask yourself:

Who are the people we intend to serve? Be as specific as possible as to age, class, income, native language, race-culture, etc.

Have we done adequate research about how various groups seek and use information, particularly about religion and values? You may think you're "open to reaching" Hispanic/Latino audience, but if your Web site's home page is in English only, and you don't offer even clues in Spanish, you are missing much of the Hispanic community.

What technologies do our current and potential customers use most readily? Can we afford to use those technologies to communicate with them?

Do the people designing and determining our technological direction understand, respect, interact with and take cues from our audience? If you are not the technological director for your communications program, push for training for your staff or contract technology folks, so that they have a basic understanding of your ethos, audiences, overall goals, and belief systems.

How do we get audience feedback? Do we continually research customer satisfaction and emerging needs?

Tailoring. If a seeker wants a simple definition of your religious/faith group, he or she can look in a dictionary or even the reliable AP Stylebook. However, I'd wager that customers who use your resources and information seek a more cultivated knowledge, a richer understanding or some "insider" information to enhance their experiences. From a novice seeking new information, to a religious leader who needs statistics or sayings from the holy book, you may have it all to give. But can seekers find what they need without excessive digging?

Again, what separates mediocre communications tools from excellent ones is usefulness to the audience, and the one-size-fits-all approach should be avoided. Most of us have learned this—at least the national level—on our Web sites. A surfer usually can find our staff directory, contact phone number and address without too much trouble. Beyond that, however, many of our search engines fall down on the job.

I was on a religious organization's site recently, searching their news archives for a release about a leader who had died within the past month. I put in his name and got about 800 hits.

Easy, right? The last one, his obituary, is right at the top of the list, right? Wrong! I scrolled 500 articles before I got to his obit. I don't know what's up with the search engine, but news releases were jumbled with old bios and announcements from his alma mater about an honorary doctoral degree he received 20 years ago. There seemed to be no logical order—not chronological anyway.

The challenge is applicable to any communication tool or system. Information should be presented to and tailored for your various users. If possible, use multiple media to get your messages across.

Back to the telephone: without stated office hours and a list of options for getting a message through, callers from across the country or around the world have no idea when to call back, to whom they should direct their queries or even if they're calling the right place.

Newsletter or magazine? Regular departments or occasional ones help guide users to information they want or need.

Signage? Passersby should be able to learn the time for worship just by looking at the sign outside your house of worship; first-time visitors should find signs and greeters available to help them find the bathroom, nursery, and worship space.

Web sites? Not only should search engines offer options to narrow the archives to be searched, but also the sites themselves should be useable by someone with an older, dial-up PC or a person with the latest desktop hot rod (many sites offer these options).

Again, for every audience you say you want to reach, you should research how they communicate, the tools they use, the methods of information retrieval they prefer—and try to meet those needs as much as possible. Better to narrow your audience and serve them well, if possible, than to do a sloppy job trying to be all things to all people.

Using Feedback. Want to know what people think of your communications plan? Ask. Ask often and ask in different ways. Ask when you make major changes in your delivery systems, whether it is redoing the layout and design of a newsletter, the look of a Web site, the announcer or format of a radio show, or the personalities on a television program.

Beyond asking, watch for clues, such as a spike in letters to the editor, a drop in customer complaints or a dip in orders for a resource. Even indifference is a clue. Silence from customers is not necessarily a good thing; just because they are not complaining, doesn't mean they like what you're doing. If yours is the only place to get a resource or information about your faith-based group, your customers may assume that mediocrity is the best you can do. Don't stand for silence. Your goal is to delight your customers, so ask them what it will take to delight them.

Customer research is a multimillion-dollar industry, and there are many cost-effective ways to do telephone, direct mail and e-mail research to determine customer opinion. In between substantive research projects, though, you can get useful customer feedback:

Do a mini survey with call-in customers. Ask customer if they would stay on the line with you another minute or two to give feedback about customer service. Ask three or four brief questions, using a satisfaction scale of 1 to 5. Do the survey for a month or so, and then tabulate the results.

Add a single customer-satisfaction question to your web site. Ask customers to rate a single feature of the site (such as a new link) or to offer feedback about a product or service ordered from the site.

Include a code number for a product discount or bonus. Add this to a direct mail or other print piece, so that if a customer calls or places an Internet order, she or he gets the bonus. This will give you some idea how widely a particular print piece was used.

A simple reminder about feedback: Don't promise what you can't or won't deliver. Professional communicators are those who have earned the trust of their customers/audiences. If you ask about the phone system and customers tell you it's terrible and you're not willing to invest in a new system, it's better not to ask at all.

If these aspects of good communications—caring, accessible, tailored, and feedback-friendly— feel familiar, it's probably because they mirror the attributes of good people skills in general. At our best, professional communicators are those who respect and want to serve others, make themselves useful and accessible, seek to offer what is needed to those who need, and respond appropriately to feedback. I call these simply the golden rules for professional communicators.

Golden rules for professional communicator

Treat each consumer like an intelligent friend whom you haven't seen in a while.

She's no dummy, but she may not share your religious beliefs or, if she does, she may not know the insider jargon and players. Write, edit, produce or publish with that "intelligent friend" image in mind. Don't talk down to consumers, but don't assume "insider" knowledge.

Think before jumping on the "tech bandwagon."

Technology is a tool to serve customer and make our work more efficient and accessible; it is a not a god that our customers have to serve. If it is not about enhancing the customer's experience with your organization–or and if it adds one scintilla of time and trouble to customers' experience with your organization, question whether this the right time for a technological upgrade.

Spend 60 percent of your time cultivating the personal relationship and 40 percent creating the systems to serve.

A former colleague described a bull-in-a-china shop coworker as having the customer-service philosophy of "Ready. Shoot. Aim." Talk with customers, assess you ability to serve them, test and retool your delivery system based on customer needs and experiences. You rarely go wrong if you keep your customer's needs near the top of your list.

II. If I Had A Hammer:
The Tools of Communicating

Chapter 3

Getting Out the News:
Communicating With Secular Journalists

By Brad Pokorny

There's an unwritten rule around newsrooms, one you won't find talked about much—or even generally acknowledged. But it's an important one for religious communicators to understand. The rule is simple: bad news is good.

The rule stems from the fact that bad news sells more papers than good news. And so, an editor who is facing a layout with mostly boring stories for the next day's paper is not very happy. But, if, suddenly, the Associated Press reports on a terrible plane crash, then the editor almost certainly feels some relief (if not a bit of guilty pleasure). Because now there will be something interesting to put on the front page. As the old saying in newsrooms goes: "If it bleeds, it leads."

It's a necessary part of a business that profits from keeping readers interested (or, if you are in broadcast, maintaining high ratings). And it's a key point that religious communicators should be aware of as they think about how best to "get out the news" about their activities.

The "bad news is good" reality underlies the fundamental tension between those on the inside of newsrooms and broadcasting studios around the world and those on the outside. Religious communicators want to spread good news. But journalists and broadcasters believe that a compelling story must have an underlying conflict or drama.

This is not to say that newspapers, magazines, and broadcast outlets don't carry good news. They do. Lots of it. You can find it on the back pages, in feature stories, reports on sporting events, the arts, and other human endeavors. And, quite often, you can find it in those parts of the paper that are devoted to religion. Indeed, journalists also know that while conflict sells papers, so does inspiration. But their first criterion is to find that sense of conflict, drama or human interest.

 Our challenge as religious communicators is to find those stories within our own congregations, faith groups, and religious communities that satisfy both concerns. We must find stories that get across our good message—and which will likely interest the ordinary person.

Understanding how to do this will help you—whether you are writing a press release, doing an interview with a secular journal, or, even, putting together your own newsletter. Because the principles that determine what makes news—or what catches human interest—are fairly universal, as is the style for writing about news.

What is news?

 News has many definitions, and virtually every journalist understands it in a slightly different way. But, in a nutshell, news is what affects other people. To take that earlier and very obvious example: a plane crash. While it directly affects those in the crash, it indirectly affects all other people who might be air travelers now or in the future, because they can easily visualize them-selves aboard that plane. But there are also commercial effects (airlines may lose business; stocks and fortunes may plummet) and questions of curiosity (how did it happen? what caused the crash?). And then there is simply the human drama of such an event. What were the life stories of those who died or survived?

In the end, really, news is about stories: stories about human beings who are doing great, daring, wonderful, evil, courageous, stupid, or oddball things. Ultimately, another best way to describe news, perhaps, is to say that it is about unusual or extraordinary things. It is also about change and transformation.

Virtually every faith group has lots of things they want to talk about to the outside world. They have meetings, prominent visitors or guests, service projects, awards, new programs, interfaith events, and/or significant speeches on issues of the day. This is part and parcel of what we wish to communicate.

But to communicate effectively—especially to the news media—you must first identify what jour-nalists call the "story angle." The story angle is that idea that indicates why and how a particular event will affect people in the wider community that quickly focuses attention on why an event is unusual or extraordinary. And finding that story angle is your job.

Finding the story angle

The place to start in developing a story is to ask the kinds of questions that a journalist will ask as he or she approaches a news event. On this point it is important to understand that journalists are generally a skeptical bunch. They are like those archetypal people from Missouri who say: "Show me." Yes, they want to write about important and unusual things, but they also want to see concrete deeds or actions—not just talk. They want to see evidence of change or transformation. With that in mind, ask yourself these kinds of questions:

- Who or how many people does the event or activity involve—and how many of them are outside your faith group? In other words, does it affect a lot of people?

- How is the event or activity different from similar events that have been done by others before? In other words, is your event unusual?

- Is there a human interest side to the story, a bit of drama? In other words, have people's lives been changed or transformed?

- What are the concrete deeds or evidence that a transformation has occurred or will occur? Can you provide statistics to back this up? In other words, is this event genuine action or just talk?

If you can answer any of these questions positively, you are on your way to finding a good story for the secular media. Your challenge, then, is to express the answer to these questions—about how your event affects lots of people or has elements of drama or is unusual—in an interesting way.

To give an imaginary example: Take the most mundane of events: the community social or potluck. How could one find an angle to make it interesting? Well, perhaps you could ask everyone to bring a dish from their country of ancestry, to celebrate our coming together out of diversity. That would make it out of the ordinary, and in that fact you could find an "angle" to pitch to the journalist. Or, at least, you've found a way to make it more likely that an editor would carry publicity about the event. Other ideas to make such an event more newsworthy might include having a notable outside speaker or tying the event to a community issue (as a fund-raiser, perhaps). Any twist can make it unusual.

Once you've figured out what the news is, the next phase in getting out the news is bringing it to the attention of the journalist. There are two primary ways to do this: a press release and/or a phone call.

The press release is used when you want to send publicity to a large number of news organizations at once, and/or when you want to include a lot of details and facts that you have already developed yourself.

A phone call can be most effective when you have a specific or urgent event, and/or you believe it will be of special interest to a specific journalist or editor or news outlet. A phone call is also useful when you hope journalists will come and do the reporting about the event themselves.

Sometimes you want to use both techniques—issuing a press release and making follow-up calls.

The press release

 A press release is basically a message to a news organization in the form of a news story. Ideally, a newspaper or magazine would be able to publish it—and/or a radio or television station would be able to read it on the air. In other words, it should be in the style of a news story, complete with an interesting lead paragraph, a number of quotes (properly attributed to a spokesperson), and concrete facts and figures about your event or activity.

The easiest and most basic style is to follow the classic "5 Ws" news style. That is, it starts with a lead paragraph that answers the basic "Who, What, Why, Where, and When" questions. The rest of the release amplifies or fills in the details on those points, sometimes also answering "How?"

Answers to these questions should be quite specific. The "who" should include the full name and title of the subject of the article; the "when," the exact date, day and time; the "where" might well include a specific street address, as well as the name of the place.

Another key point: it is important, unless you are just trying to announce a brief event for a newspaper's calendar of events section, to include a quote or two or more from someone in your organization. Quotes give the story life—and they are an important part of the "show me" mentality. They show that a concrete person or thing has said something, not merely a disembodied organization. And since journalists would normally want to use a quote or two in a story they would write, the availability of quotes make it more likely such a release will be used.

In terms of writing style, keep your sentences and paragraphs short. Put your most important details at the top of the release, with less important information at the bottom. It is important to do this because news organizations rarely publish an entire news release. They will cut it from the bottom. So you want to ensure the most important information survives. This is called the "pyramid" style of focusing a news story: the "point" of the story is on top, and the rest of the ideas support that point.

As you write your release, go back over it several times and ask yourself: "What is the most important point" and "what is the most interesting point?" Sometimes in the writing of it, you will see that some other point you thought was less important is, in fact, the most interesting aspect. Also be sure to carefully proofread your release for correct spelling (especially for names and places) and for grammatical errors.

Be sure to label the story as a press release and include detailed information on how to contact you or someone in your organization for more details. You should list office, home and even cell phone numbers, as well as e-mail addresses. If the journalists decide to use the release, they may want to contact you for more information (indeed, getting them to interview you is often a major goal of issuing a release)—and so you must make it as easy as possible for them to contact you.

It is also helpful to have a suggested headline, something short and catchy, like any good newspaper headline.

If the release is mailed out, it should be on your group's letterhead. If sent out by e-mail, it is best just to send it as plain text. In other words, don't send the formatted release as a file attachment, because it is just another barrier to the journalists: it requires more time for them to consider it and there is also the concern of computer viruses. If, however, you need to send special images or formatting, it is okay to send attached files, as long as you explain what the attachments are in plain text.

 One way to get ideas about how to write news releases is to read releases put out by other groups and organizations. For religious communicators, perhaps the best source for such releases is the World Faith News site on the World Wide Web at www.wfn.org. This not-for-profit, interfaith site carries national and international news releases by most of the major faith groups in the USA, and, to some extent around the world.

Where to send your release

Writing the release is half the job. The other half is getting it delivered to the person in a news organization who will be most likely to read it and use it. In many large cities in the United States, newspapers now have specialists who cover religion exclusively. You should make it a point to know who these writers are and to have a ready list of their names, addresses, phone numbers, and e-mail addresses.

In smaller cities and towns, it is likely that you will simply send your release to the "editor" of each news outlet in town and let them decide who should consider it.

You should also carefully read your local newspapers (and watch or listen to local broadcasts) and identify journalists who seem to be writing about the types of stories you are promoting. In many cities and towns, religious communicators have the best luck with columnists who are free to write about whatever events or ideas interest them in the region.

Ultimately, you should develop a database of journalists and broadcasters in your area.

Talking to Journalists

Sometimes your news is so urgent or specialized that the best way to get it out is to call a reporter or editor directly. As well, you must be prepared for what to say when and if the journalists call you for more information.

The newsletter of the Bahá'í International Community
866 United Nations Plaza, Suite 120
New York, NY 10017

Use your organization's letterhead whenever possible

PRESS RELEASE
For immediate release
Release date: 26 March 2004
For more information, contact: Brad Pokorny, 212-803-2500; mobile: 603-867-6676

Identify it as a press release, indicate when the release is dated and when it can be used

Always provide a person to contact and include work and after-hours phone numbers

**ONE COUNTRY wins Award of Excellence
from Religious Communicators Council**

The dateline tells what city the event takes place in

Headlines should be boldface, short and catchy

BIRMINGHAM, Alabama — ONE COUNTRY, the newsletter of the Bahá'í International Community, received an Award of Excellence from the Religion Communicators Council (RCC) at ceremonies here on 26 March 2004.

The first paragraph summarizes the five "W"s -- who, what, where, when, and why

The award, in the newspaper features category, was given for a story titled "In Vanuatu, a proving ground for coconut oil as alternative fuel," which was published in the April-June 2003 issue.

The second paragraph should add detail and explanation

"We are gratified to be recognized by our colleagues in this way," said Brad Pokorny, editor of ONE COUNTRY. "So often, as editors and reporters, we toil away without knowing whether our words are being well received."

The use of quotations from real people gives the release life and makes it more engaging

The awards, known as the DeRose-Hinkhouse awards, were presented at the Council's annual convention, held this year in Birmingham.

The awards recognize the achievements of RCC members who demonstrate excellence in their fields. Entries in various categories are judged by peers in local chapters across the country. The awards honor the late Victor DeRose and Paul M. Hinkhouse, leading lithographers in New York City.

Somewhere in the release it should explain why this news is important, perhaps through a quote

Other pargraphs flesh out the "W"s — giving more on why, what or how

"These awards validate the imagination and originality so plentiful in our RCC family," said Ronald T. Glusenkamp, chair of the DeRose-Hinkhouse awards and vice president of customer outreach for the Evangelical Lutheran Church of America Board of Pension in Minneapolis. "They demonstrate the high quality of work that institutions receive from our RCC members."

The award-winning story tells of the efforts of Tony Deamer, a Bahá'í on the South Pacific island of Vanuatu, to invent and promote a new technology that makes it feasible to operate diesel automobiles on coconut oil instead of petroleum, which will help protect the environment.

- end -

It is standard procedure to indicate the end of the release

In such communications with journalists, keep in mind that they are generally very busy—and so their attention span is limited. You must be ready to make the main points about your message quickly. Specifically, you should be able to say why it is an important story in the first 30 seconds of your call.

At the same time, understand that journalists do want news. They want to be informed about what is happening in the community they cover. So you should not be shy about making quick calls if you have a story or activity that you believe will be of interest.

It is important to be prepared for follow-up questions. Most reporters are generalists, and they don't have a lot of in-depth knowledge about any one particular subject. Your attitude should be one of helpfulness and service. Keep these points in mind:

Know your facts and everything about the event. This might include biographical details about prominent speakers or panelists, carefully developed data about the impact of a project or community outreach, and/or general socio-economic statistics about an area that is to be served.

Develop a list of other people the journalist can contact or call. This list should include spokespeople from your own organization, of course, but it might also include people who are not members of your faith group, but who are knowledgeable about the activity or project. Such spokespeople will give you added credibility.

Prepare a list of "talking points" or "positive points." Such talking points might be based on your press release—but they would include short, positive, conversational points that, again, answer those key questions about why an event is newsworthy. They would stress its benefits for the wider community, its distinctive approach or impact, and/or its human interest angle.

 If you land an interview, or engage in a longer conversation about your story or event, keep in mind the following:

Listen carefully to the questions. Don't jump the gun with poorly thought-out answers.

Give short, concise answers. They are more easily quoted. And, especially, don't go into a long discussion of points that the reporter has not asked about.

Speak in full sentences. Journalists can't easily quote from sentence fragments. Also, try not to shift thoughts in mid-stream. Finish one idea and move on to another in your conversation. (In normal conversation, people often shift thoughts two or three times without completing a sentence. In context, your listener will know what you mean. But in a newspaper quote, it won't make sense.)

Avoid the use of jargon and specialized terms. No doubt, your faith group has specific terminology—and sometimes acronyms—for its governing bodies, practices, and theological concepts. Avoid the use of these terms and instead explain things in ordinary language, as if you were speaking to someone who knows nothing about your group.

Chapter 4

Graphic Identity:
Do You Know Who You Are? Do They?

By Nancy Fisher and Jay Sidebotham

What is graphic identity, anyway?

Your graphic identity is your "face." It is one of the ways you communicate with your constituents, clients, and members. Like all communications, your graphic identity should be:

On strategy

(Of course, this assumes you have a corporate strategy. If not, that would be a good place to start.)

Appropriate for the target market

(Of course, this assumes you have defined and understood your target market. If not... well, you get the idea.) Here's an example of the importance of thinking about your target market before you start your graphic design process, and then fully briefing the designer. A multi-denominational association that shall remain nameless decided to add a logo to its letterhead. Since the name of the organization included the word "church," the design firm came up with a number of interesting logo designs that incorporated a church topped by a cross. It was only after the association reviewed the designs and selected several "finalist" logos that somebody said, "Hey, several of our member organizations are Jewish!" No one had mentioned this fact to the design firm. Back to the drawing board!

Said in a new, interesting, motivating way

Face it. Many people come to religious services or read religious publications expecting to be bored. In the secular setting, communicators are always searching for that new idea, or a new way of presenting an old idea. Religious communicators have not always done that. So if you can find a way to do that, you've got a great advantage. You'll find people are pleasantly surprised. One church did this by buying an ad on the religious services pages, where all the other congregations listed their services using the most technical religious language (for example: "solemn evensong," "choral Eucharist"). This church had an artist draw a shopping cart with a church in it, a simple, bold line drawing that leapt off the page, in an appeal to church shoppers. It's an example of approaching religious communication in a new way. You can do that, too.

Executed with excellence

Your graphic identity is not just your logo. It's everything you put out there—letterhead, signage, brochures, advertising, PowerPoint. It's the fonts you use, how the words look on the page, the colors you use. It's also the style of your communications—illustrations, charts, graphics—and their spirit—humor, for example, or poignancy, or a sense of mission. Consistency in your visual look is achieved through standardization. Therefore, graphic identity standards must be specifically defined. However, this should not mean that creativity is stifled. Flexibility and choice must be built into your graphic standards, to allow for wide range of creativity under a unifying design "umbrella."

How do you evaluate your graphic identity?

Know thyself. Who do you think you are? How are you perceived by your clients? Be intentional: Is who you are who you want to be?

Consider undertaking an identity analysis. There are professionals who can guide you. Or you can attempt it yourself—as long as you can be dispassionate in your research.

 Start with a self-discovery process in which you conduct in-depth, one-on-one interviews with a cross-section of senior and middle management people, as well as your constituents where indicated, around specific questions and issues.

Define changing business climates and factors that affect your organization.

Define the organization's broad objectives.

> **Examples:** "We should maintain and grow our leadership position." "We should increase the range of products and services we offer." "We should show how good we are at what we do." "We should be leaders in outreach ministries." "Our message should reach a lot more people."

Perform a corporate philosophy/mission/values audit. Ask questions both of internal staff and your constituents. What are the company's/organization's perceived strengths and weaknesses? What associations do people have with it?

> **Examples:** "We started out by helping people, and that's still the most important thing we do today." "Spirituality is the basis of our success." "We're about service, not products."

Be honest; make sure you hear the negatives as well as the positives.

> **Example:** "We are viewed as paternalistic and complacent."
>
> You might also want to talk with people who are new to the community. It's been said that the newest in-law in a family has the best read on that family and its dynamics. That can be true in congregations, and in religious communications. Ask the opinion of those who are new to the community, or even better, those who may never have set foot in the place. You'll flatter them as you seek their wisdom, and you may learn something.

Define the competition and the importance of differentiating yourself from others.

> **Examples:** "Our competition has more sophisticated marketing practices." "We provide better service." "Once people understand who we really are, they respect and trust us. But I have to spend half of every presentation explaining who we are." "Clear identity communication will help us stand out." "People don't know about all the volunteer opportunities we offer."

Define the target audiences and the appropriate message(s) for each.

> **Examples:**
>
> | | |
> |---|---|
> | churches | programs/service/heritage |
> | clergy and lay employees | quality/care/service |
> | the press | news/heritage/reliability |

Determine how the company or organization should be positioned in the future, given both its business objectives and the ways in which it is currently perceived.

> **Examples:** "We should appear to be on an equal footing with our competition." "As long as you say 'church,' people will assume the rest." "Although we have various chapters, we need to present ourselves as a unified whole." "There have been some bad experiences in the past. We want people to realize we've moved beyond that and have improved."

Perform a communications audit. Lay everything out on the table and look at it. What sorts of pieces do you generally produce: posters, annual reports, brochures, newsletters, advertising? Is that likely to change? What is the overall impact of your communications? How can your clients tell that the materials they receive from you are from you? Given the business and social climates, your objectives, philosophy and mission, and the way management feels that the company or organization should be positioned for the future, is your current graphic identity doing the job? (Also, see chapter one).

So you need a new or updated identity!

Having completed your self-discovery process, the next step is to perform a graphics analysis study. It's important to involve those same middle and senior management people—and others, if relevant—in this study, too. Acceptance of a new graphic identity and adherence to new graphic standards only work if management buys into it, and buy-in is created through corporate leadership involvement in analysis and decision-making.

Elicit from senior- and middle-management people what they perceive to be the most significant issues facing the organization in regard to the current graphic identity and possible changes to it.

> **Examples:** "We have a number of affiliates/chapters and they all look different. We aren't perceived as one organization." "We have no identity presence." "Any new identity should reflect the pride we take in what we provide to our members." "Our symbol/logo doesn't relate to who we are today." "Will our constituents recognize us if we change our logo/the way our materials look?"

Understand the challenges inherent in clarifying your image and presenting an understandable, high-quality identity to the people you serve.

> **Examples:** Reaching consensus regarding the character of the new identity. Getting buy-in from management. Making a commitment to a long-term sustained effort to establish and maintain new graphic standards.

Make a list of company/organization strengths and weaknesses, drawn from conversations with internal and external sources. Use adjectives or short phrases rather than descriptive sentences.

> **Examples:** successful; progressive; understand needs; responsive; techno-savvy; well-managed; churchlike; integrity; good name, VERSUS lack of presence in market/community; viewed as old-fashioned; look of communications unrelated to what we do; no consistent messages.

Make a two-column list of "current" versus "desired" image attributes. These will form the basis of the design criteria.

Example:

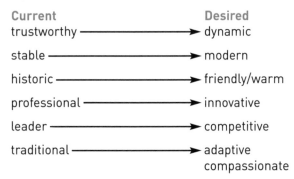

Current	Desired
trustworthy ⟶	dynamic
stable ⟶	modern
historic ⟶	friendly/warm
professional ⟶	innovative
leader ⟶	competitive
traditional ⟶	adaptive
	compassionate

Include verbatims: significant spontaneous remarks made by people during the interview process.

List any symbols already associated with your organization. What does each connote? How does that connotation complement or fight against what you have now learned about your corporate identity?

The learnings from your self-discovery process and graphics analysis study should be captured in a written document that should also contain "conclusions and recommendations" and "preliminary design criteria" sections. This document should directly inform the actual graphic design process.

Logo or no-go?

Does everyone need a logo?

Often, people who are not sure of how to discover and implement a graphic identity immediately assume they need a logo. But where is it written that all religious organizations must have a logo? Logos can be helpful, providing a way to tie together many communications and efforts. But there are many ways that can be accomplished through graphic design alone Logos should never be used as an easy fix for the lack of a graphic identity, or as a substitute for good graphic design.

Using multiple logos within a single company or organization can also be counter-productive. One religious communicator working in a large congregation found that every group (altar guild, soup kitchen, urban ministry, inquirer's class) wanted its own logo. It was as if each group felt that its work did not mean much without it. But 'branding' every group in a single organization will only serve to diffuse—and confuse—that organization's overall identity.

A logo should be simple, tasteful, engaging. Like many simple things, it's not always arrived at easily. It can take work and exploration to design a logo—it's best not done by committee—and once you've selected a design, it's important to stick with it. It can be abstract. It can be representational. It can depict some aspect of the community (a steeple, a geographic setting). It can simply evoke a spirit. Usually, you know a good logo when you see one.

Some years back, the story was told of a company designing a new logo, an abstract "N." It was presented to one group of executives who received it with acclaim. "We like it because it says 'N' loud and clear," they said. "No mistaking it." Pleased, the designers proceeded to the next level for approval, where it also received acclaim. "We like it because it doesn't shout 'N,'" they were told. "It takes you a while to see it." Just goes to show that a good design is often in the eye of the beholder.

Once the logo has been designed and embraced by the community, avoid the temptation to change it, add to it, or use it in conjunction with other logos. Maintaining logo integrity is important in helping the logo to do the work it was designed to do.

Identify yourself!

Logos are not the only way to consistently identify yourself to your audience. The use of visual identifiers can do the same thing. Identifiers are visual elements that, when used consistently, identify each piece as having come from your company or organization. As part of its recent graphic redesign, the Church Pension Group created a graphic identifier by using the right side of its shield symbol—a symbol that has long been associated with CPG and is part of its redesigned logo. This graphic identifier can be used as an outline, a solid, or a background, and in a variety of sizes, thus allowing for a wide range of graphic expressions all of which incorporate a unifying graphic element. Several examples appear below.

Graphic design is not as easy as it looks.
The sophisticated graphic design tools available today make it possible for everyone to do it. But not everyone can do it well. So hire a professional designer on a freelance/consulting basis to set templates that can then be followed by in-house or office staff. Or, if you can't afford that, try to recruit professionals who are members of your faith group or wider religious community to volunteer their time and talent. Painting the garage is a great do-it-yourself project; creating a graphic identity is not.

Breaking through the clutter
We're all bombarded by a clutter of communications every day: in our mail boxes, on television, on billboards and signs, via e-mail and the Internet. So it's important not only that your communications

stand out, but that they look like you. Here's an example of graphic 'thinking' that really works. Through the consistent use of recognizable typography and drawings, St. Bartholomew's Church, in New York City, has created a friendly, accessible, identifiable graphic image. Several examples of their communications appear below.

Not every kid wants the same kind of camp. And we want happy campers. That's why Summer CATS* at St. Bart's is offering three options:

St. Bart's Day Camp • June 21–August 27
Perfect for 3 1/2 year to 9 year olds: swimming every day, sports, martial and circus arts, dance plus a whole lot more on our rooftop playground!

Island Sports Camp • June 21–August 27
For 6-11 year olds who like something a little more sporty. Start the day with swimming instruction in St. Bart's indoor pool then jet off to Roosevelt Island for a day of softball, soccer, tennis and (on rainy days) indoor sports.

Travel Camp • July 12–August 20
Created for 8-12 year olds with a sense of adventure. Each day campers will travel to a different educational or recreational site in the area. Swimming and sports, too!

Summer CATS at St. Bart's also offers flexible scheduling and an After Camp program. To register, schedule a family tour at your convenience or to receive more information, contact Jamie Martin Currie at 212-378-0203, martincurrie@stbarts.org or look on our website: www.stbarts.org.

*CATS (Children's Athletic Training School) is the first and only comprehensive children's sports training program in the country for children ages 1-12. Summer CATS at St. Bart's is located at 109 E. 50th Street in Manhattan.

Come to St. Bart's: the camp, not the island.

Now you can sleep through Sunday Services and still stay in good graces.

Come as you are to the 7pm Service at St. Bart's.

Why not do your sleeping before church instead of during it. Come to the evening service at St. Bart's. You'll find a whole new kind of music, liturgy and fellowship. And of course, there's free child care, coffee afterwards and a very relaxed dress code. So unplug the alarm and join us.

Park Avenue at 51st Street, New York City. 212-378-0200 www.stbarts.org

Miracle on 50th Street: A Modern Day Christmas Story

An original play written by St. Bart's youth and performed by children of the parish.

Saturday, December 20 at 3pm & 4pm • Free St. Bartholomew's Church Park Avenue at 51st Street, New York City

Call 212-378-0222 or email central@stbarts.org for reservations.

Summary

The key is to discover and define who you are, whom you wish to reach, and what you want people to take away from your communications. That process of discovery can be a wonderfully inclusive endeavor, allowing you to talk to people both within and outside of the community. Then become as clear as you can about the work your community feels called to do, and see how you can shape an identity that can be embraced and preserved in order to further that work. It can be a challenging undertaking. Graphic identity is indeed a subjective enterprise. But along with that challenge comes the promise that your efforts to be clear about your identity and the ways you convey that identity will strengthen your community and further your endeavors. It's worth it.

Chapter 5

Get the Picture?

By Bret Haines

Let's begin with five different scenarios that will happen to you—if they haven't already:

Scenario One:
You have just been handed seven photos taken of a Volunteers-in-Mission team that visited a foreign country. All of them are of the team standing shoulder to shoulder in front of a brick wall. They are smiling and posing for the camera. They would have looked exactly the same if they had they been photographed in your backyard.

Scenario Two:
You get a call from someone in another city. They want a copy of the logo for an event your annual conference is doing. You e-mail them the graphic file you use to promote the event. Ten minutes later they call back saying they can't open the document and they ask you to reformat it. You do so only to find out the size of the document is now too large to e-mail. You send it Fed Ex on a CD to them. The next day they call and tell you that they can't use this one either and ask you if the file might be corrupt. You spend 30 minutes troubleshooting the problem over the phone and determine that the software they are using is the problem. You reformat the logo one more time, send it on a new disc and get a call over the weekend because they realize they need the logo in black and white and not color.

Scenario Three:
You buy a digital camera. You are expected to photograph several visiting district superintendents who will only be in town briefly. You get the photo you need (at least you think you did) and now need to transfer it to your computer. But how?

Scenario Four:
You are given a photograph that needs to be scanned for your next newsletter. The photo is a wallet size mug shot and you scan it at the same size. You return the photo and after a month begin to lay out your newsletter. Now, however, you realize you need the photo to be much larger. When you enlarge it to fit the space it looks all "stair-steppy."

Scenario Five:
Somebody hands you a disc with a file on it. They will tell you that it is a photo of Bishop So-and-so and it's supposed to go in your newspaper. What they have handed you will be one of 11 different file types, in one of six different modes, in one of three different formats, saved in one of two different computer platforms, on one of 10 different kinds of media.

Of course, there are more scenarios, but—pardon the pun—you get picture. This chapter will help you determine how to use illustrative materials—such as photography, illustrations, logos, and other graphics—in the communication tools you produce. You will also learn how to specify the kind of art you need, in exactly the format you need, on the kind of media that you need. Let's start with the basics.

Selecting and using photographs

You've heard and experienced that a picture is worth a thousand words. However, we should qualify that statement a bit. A *good* picture is worth a thousand words. The bad picture, however, is one that needs a thousand words to help explain it. Specifically, the photograph (and its caption) should be selected and used to enhance the message of the article (or poster, brochure, etc.). An action shot of that mission team that went to Africa would have gone much farther than any posed photo. Better still, several action shots would do wonders for the readership of any publication.

The unfortunate reality is that when people see the camera pointed in their direction, in true Pavlovian style, they are conditioned to line up and smile. It can't hurt to have a shot like that (sometimes you absolutely must have those grinning heads), but keep shooting after the group shot has been captured. Your subjects will very likely return to doing whatever they were doing before the Kodak moment happened and that is where you will find the real opportunities.

There will be times when all you have is what someone gives you. There are tricks to make the best of it. Eliminate the background using some photo-manipulation software like Adobe Photoshop. By removing the unnecessary brick wall from behind the group and just using the people in the shot you add visual interest to that posed photograph. Also, many people who give you a photo may not know any better; they might have great action photos that they have not shown you. Ask if you can see all the photos from the event. There might just be a gem in there that will be the perfect opening shot.

Digital photography

The digital camera is an amazing tool that can knock days off of your imaging process and can save you money by eliminating developing, film, and print costs. However, if you are like an easily-startled, woodland creature when it comes to technology, then here are the considerations that go into selecting a digital camera. (See CD for glossary of terms)

Mega pixels: You don't need to know what they are. All you need to know is more is better. Don't plan on getting anything below 2.0 mega pixels because you won't like the image quality. A 2.5 mega pixel camera will produce a perfectly fine 5 by 7 image suitable for any newsletter publication. The higher the mega pixel the bigger the image you can reproduce successfully.

What do you need the camera for? If you are shooting for your Web page only, then you won't need a high mega pixel camera. Spend your money on a 2.0 camera with better zoom features or lightweight size or more storage options. If you are shooting for print publications, spend more dollars for more mega pixels. Photos for printed material need more image information than Web graphics so the file sizes will be larger. If you are just using the digital camera to make prints for your scrap book, then try to find a camera/printer combination. Some cameras and printers are intended to be used together and are designed to print snap-shot like images for your photo album.

How do you get the image on your computer? The first step is to know what kind of connectivity options your computer has. Is it an older computer that will not accept new connections? Is it a newer, speedier computer with the latest technology? Check your computer user's manual to find out before you look for cameras. It may save you money and hassle in the end.

Similarly, many cameras on the market come with built in memory and can store up to hundreds of images. Others use removable storage media. But if you can't get them out of the camera you may have to invest in other options. Sony cameras have memory sticks so you may have to spend a hundred or so dollars on a memory stick reader if you can't connect the camera directly to your computer. Other media include Smartcards and Compact Flash Cards. Storage media can be purchased in various megabyte sizes; the higher the megs on a card, the more photos you can shoot. Just be sure you have a way to get pictures on your computer before you buy any camera.

What kind of camera should you get? Many trade publications like MacWorld and Consumer Reports rank the latest technology regularly. See what they say about the newest camera comparisons. Make certain you know the features you need: 4.0 mega pixels, long-distance zoom, pocket size, lightweight, USB connection, and all the software for your particular computer, etc. Then see which camera will fulfill your needs.

Art files, graphics, and scans, oh my!

Way back in the old days. . . . well, no, actually, we are just talking about the 80s. But back then, art—whether it was photography, illustration, or graphics—was provided on a separate paste-up and given to the printer to place into the film for you. The graphic artist would specify where the art was to go and the size and the printer handled the rest. The people who handled that part of the job were called (don't laugh) strippers. They would "strip" the artwork into film overlays and burn the plates necessary to print the job.

Now, thanks to Apple Computers, Microsoft, Adobe, and thousands of graphic designers who demanded more control, the person doing the layout has the task of getting that layout organized with all of the graphic elements in place, thus sending most strippers into other careers. All that is to say that you were never supposed to fret about all of the technical worries that are associated with this process. But, until it becomes easier, here is what you need to know in order to publish materials with art works and graphics.

Rule number 1: Know the software for which the scan is intended. If you are creating your layouts in Microsoft Word, then you need to know the kind of scan that will work in Word. The same can be said for other composition applications: WordPerfect, Publisher, InDesign, and QuarkXPress. Each software package will accept a variety of graphic or scan formats. Not all formats will agree with every package. And not every file type is going to work for the kind of publishing you have in mind. For print purposes, your software should let you know how to import graphic files and the file types that work best.

How do you know which files to use and when? Knowing the answer to this is the key to getting the best image quality for your publication, print or Web.

The first thing to know is the difference between the two main graphic formats for graphics: *raster* and *vector*.

The *raster* file is used mostly for your photographs but all of your graphics can be rasterized. The benefit is increased usability. The drawbacks to raster files are several: You should know the correct size of the final scan and have the file saved at that size. You also need to be rather specific about the resolution of the image. A low resolution file, like most files used for the Web, will be blurry when they go to print. Typically, a high resolution file—anywhere from 200dpi to 300dpi when the image is reproduced at 100 percent—is the best choice for print. You also need to be exacting about whether the image will be used in color or grayscale.

Let's use an example: you have a full color brochure and you have an image selected for the cover. The cover measures 8.5" high and 3.5" wide. Your photo is a vertical 5" by 7" image. The application you are using to layout the brochure is QuarkXPress. What you need is to scan the 7" size of the photo to slightly larger than 8.5" high (to accommodate for bleeding off the page). The scan, therefore, will have the following specs: the size will be 300 dpi at about 122 percent of the original size. The image will be scanned in CMYK mode for the four-color printing process (RGB mode is mostly for Web usage). The resulting rasterized image will then be saved in a graphic format for use in Quark; either a TIFF file or an EPS. If you are not sure about how to calculate these specifications, your printer should be able to help.

The other file format is called a *vector*. The vector file is used for graphics such as logos, charts, graphs, etc. Wherever "flat color" or Pantone color is used instead of images will be a good place for vector art. The benefits of using vector art? Versatility in image size is one of the biggest benefits. Unlike raster images, an inch wide vector image can be enlarged to billboard size without losing any detail. The file size is much smaller, too. Raster files are memory hungry. Vector files are graphics created with "paths" which hold all of the color and shape information. Raster images are made up of pixels; the larger the image, the more pixels are needed to "draw" the image. The more pixels, the more your memory needs increase. The drawback to using the vector file is that many applications (especially older version numbers of many popular applications) do not support the .eps format, which is the most common way to save the vector file.

The EPS (.eps) is a file type that can be either vector or raster. It stands for "Encapsulated PostScript," a graphic computer language that works well on Macintosh computers and is slowly gaining more compatibility in the Windows environment. Other file types which work well for print media that you can use for saving your files are TIFF and BMP formats. The TIFF (.tif) stands for Tagged Image File Format and is probably the most versatile. You can save four-color, grayscale, and solid black-and-white raster graphics using the TIFF format. The BMP, or Bitmap graphic, is a Microsoft product and works well with Microsoft applications. Here again, the key to knowing the difference to these formats is knowing which graphic your application likes best. Check your user's manual or ask your printing representative for help.

There are many more file formats for saving graphics. If you are getting art from an outside source be sure you know if you need a raster image (for photos) or vector (for logos); then specify the file type, the size you need, the resolution at that size, color or grayscale, and (especially if you are a Windows user) the computer platform. This tip will save you a lot of trouble getting the right graphic for your needs.

Use graphics from the Web

The Web can be a great source for art. Many Websites provide copyright-free images that can be reproduced without a fee. Other sites provide commercial, stock images that can be purchased for a fee that is calculated on usage. Typically, the usage fee for most of these images is for one-time only. The fees also go higher depending upon how the image will be used (cover art for instance), the size (full page vs. half page or smaller), circulation, and intent (to sell products vs. promoting a non-profit service). Many prices can be negotiated and it doesn't hurt to mention that the images will be used in a faith-related publication. Special rates and compensations exist for non-profits, so take advantage of them!

Also, The United Methodist Church has many opportunities for collecting images. The various boards and agencies keep photographic records, logo and image libraries, and photo galleries where images can be downloaded and used for free. One great source for this is the United Methodist News Service Webpage at www.umns.umc.org and The United Methodist Church Web site at www.umc.org. Check there for logos, art, and photos—you won't be sorry!

Image 1

Image 2

Image 3

Image 4

The group photo

There is no avoiding the "group shot" but there are things to be aware of when you are getting it. **Image 1** is the worst kind of photo (don't laugh, someone will hand you one just like this someday). You can argue that it accomplishes the goal of getting the group together for identification purposes, but is it worth a thousand words? Contrast it with **Image 2**, of an Alternate Spring Break group from a campus ministry at Vanderbilt University. Everyone is looking at the camera and can be identified with a caption. But the background gives you a hint about the group's trip to Mexico and adds visual interest to the shot. The group in Image 1 could have been somewhere interesting, but the photo gives you no other information. It is dull and lifeless.

Other things you should be aware of are in Images 3 and 4. In **Image 3**, be aware of what is going on in the rest of the photo. The woman receiving her award is being upstaged by the fact that the others in the photo were not aware that the picture was being made. A little cropping can make up for a photographer's mistake.

In **Image 4**, we have a student group visiting London. Whether you are taking the photo or using it in your publication, be aware of the content. For instance, a faith group publication may not be the best place for the beer ad in the background (did you catch it?) or the "thumbs up" gesture in the foreground (in some cultures, this gesture can be considered offensive).

Finally, don't confuse these files with the images that are used to decorate someone's Web page. The graphics and photos that adorn many homepages are low resolution images specifically formatted for Web use. Resolution, again, is the key here. Web images are typically 72dpi at 100 percent of their intended size. Print images need to be anywhere from 200dpi to 300dpi. Using a low resolution Web image will result in poor print quality. This is often characterized as being "pixelated" or "stair-stepped" because of the visible block patterns and rough edges typical of low resolution images.

Evaluate the use of your images

Evaluate your images by: appropriateness to the subject, visual/verbal synergy, content, clarity, and cropping.

The appropriateness criterion can be the most subjective—especially when using the images in an editorial context. Ask yourself: Does the image contain inappropriate content in the background (alcohol or cigarette ads, lewd gestures, graffiti, etc.)? Does it show people in stereotypical, racist, or sexist contexts? Or was the sun so bright that day that all persons with dark complexions become formless shadows while light complexion persons "burn-out" completely? And, finally, does the image really go with the article?

Visual/verbal synergy is when the headline, callout, or other descriptive copy says one thing and the image shows another, but when used together can express a more complete idea. An example might be a headline for your article about your church's Christmas service entitled "Hark, the Herald Angels Sing!" The hymn title makes a nice headline and has connotations all its own. But if you couple it with an action shot of the children's choir singing, then synergy is created. The headline takes on a whole new meaning—a meaning it might not otherwise have had without the image.

Content has to do with the activity in the image. Here again, action shots are much better than group photos. If you have both, feature the group photo smaller and the action shot larger. It will add visual interest to your layout and increase the number of readers.

Clarity in your image has as much to do with "what is going on" as it does with focus, appropriate lighting, and composition. The best solution to this issue is to recruit a good photographer, but selecting images that match the content of the written copy is just as important.

When all else fails, cropping can improve a poorly composed image. My rule of thumb usually is to remove all items in the photo that do not contribute to the story. If I have a shot of the children's choir singing in the middle of the sanctuary, I crop in to the shoulders of the outside children and down to just above the head of the tallest kid in the back row. All of the peripheral information around them (the pulpit on the right, the exit door on the left, the microphones hanging from the ceiling) contribute nothing and just don't need to be in the image. This also allows me to make the most of the image by enlarging the action!

The Final Frame

The tips in this chapter should help you deal with the scenarios described at the beginning. In a day and age when your audience—and especially the youth—are visually savvy, it is important to keep your publications visually interesting. Hundreds of messages compete for your attention each day; from the box design of your breakfast cereal, to the dozens of ads in your city newspaper, to the barrage of images that pour from the television, video games, and computer screen. Make no mistake; your publication competes with them all. So make the best of it by using photography that catches your own eye. Your audience will be grateful!

Chapter 6

Design: Do It Yourself Demo

By Kami Lund and Linda Svensk

Have you ever received a print publication you found hard to read? Was it because the type size was too small? Was the amount of text on the page intimidating? Was the publication's message hidden behind a glitzy design filled with color and graphics?

To produce an appealing newsletter, brochure or other print publication, your information needs to be in an easy-to-read, eye-catching format. Experience tells us that a well-designed publication is more effective in getting news and messages out to the masses. Taking the time to understand and follow simple fundamentals of design will result in a publication that is easy to read, easy to understand and pleasing to view.

To create a publication that fits the needs of your readers, you first must define and understand your audience:

What common interest does your audience share? Are your readers members of the same faith community or organization? Do they participate in the same group or activity?

What are your audience's characteristics? Big or small? Older or younger? Male or female?

What does your audience need? Quick information? In-depth, detailed information?

Your audience will help determine your publication's content, layout, timing and methods of reproduction and distribution.

You also need to determine the purpose or mission of your publication. Newsletters and brochures can be used to help

- inform
- educate
- persuade
- promote or sell
- boost morale
- increase productivity
- solicit financial support

The purpose or mission of your publication should be specific. Your message will get lost if you try to cover too many unrelated topics in one publication.

Newsletter design elements

In addition to articles, your newsletter should include:

- a banner or nameplate—the name of your newsletter, publication date, and its issue or volume number on the front page

- table of contents—if your newsletter is more than two pages long

- masthead—the newsletter editor and organization's contact and copyright information (usually on the second or last page)

- headlines—used to announce your stories

- subheads—smaller headlines within stories to break up the text and add white space

- photos or graphics related to the content to draw interest

Newsletter size

A newsletter can be a single page or have multiple pages. The easiest paper size to work with is 8.5" by 11" (standard letter-sized paper). If you will have a four- or eight-page newsletter, you may want to consider printing it on 11" by 17" paper and folding it in half to create the 8.5" by 11" document.

Layout basics

After your audience is defined and your articles are written and edited, it's time to begin the production phase of your publication. Though it may be fun to use the variety of colors, graphics and fonts offered with many design tools, remember, readability is the most important aspect of your piece. Everything else should be used to enhance the text. If your message is lost behind your graphical elements, your publication will be less effective.

An easy-to-read publication uses

- a serif font for text and a sans serif font for headlines and subheads

    serif fonts have small extra strokes at the end of the lines that form the letters

    sans serif fonts have no extra strokes at the end of the lines that form the letters

- a type size of 11 points or larger

- contrasting colors—black text on white or light-colored paper

- white space (empty or blank space on the page that gives the reader's eye a break)

- margins that are left aligned rather than justified

- text in columns and boxes

- related stories grouped together on a page

- graphics or photos that visually describe the story and draw interest

Font, typestyle and size

Studies on publication readability have shown that

- serif fonts are easier to read in blocks of text than sans serif fonts

- lowercase letters are easier to read than all uppercase letters

- Italicized or bold blocks of text are hard to read

- Headlines in bold text catch the reader's attention

Additionally, at different ages, people prefer different type sizes. For your general readership, type should be set at 11 or 12 points. For older people and people with visual impairments, 14 point type or larger may be appropriate. Consider your audience's needs to determine the size of type you use in your publication.

It is acceptable to use up to three fonts in your publication—one for text, one for headlines, and one for your banner or nameplate. Using more than three may make your publication appear busy and unrelated.

Serif and sans serif fonts

This is Times New Roman. This is a serif font.

This is Palatino. This is a serif font

This is Arial. This is a sans serif font.

This is Verdana. This is a sans serif font.

Headlines

Headlines are used to grab attention, tell your reader what the accompanying story is about and make your reader stay interested enough to read the story. Your reader should be able to pick up on the main news or topics in your newsletter by quickly scanning the headlines.

Headlines should always be placed above the articles they introduce. Additionally, because headlines are essential to the readability and look of your publication, try to make use of the full space you have allotted for them. Note: A period is not needed after a headline.

Headline sizes can range from 14 points to 30 points, depending on your layout and space constraints. Generally, stories set at the top of the page (or more important stories) have a larger-sized headline than stories set lower on the page (or less important stories). Note: It is important to keep your headline sizes consistent throughout your publication. Select a size for important stories and select a size for less important stories and stick with it. Or, use the same size headline for every story.

Things to avoid:

colored text on colored paper (e.g., blue ink on blue paper)

red or yellow text

reverse text (white text with a black or dark background)

justified   text   (the   block   of   text   lined   up   on   the   right   edge)

"watermark" images (printing text over pictures or images—
this is distracting to the reader)

more than two fonts for text and headlines **within your publication**

blocks of bolded or italicized text

The benefits of white space

Many beginning designers may think that every inch of the page must be covered with text or graphics. This is not the case at all. The use of "white space," the space on the page that is not occupied by any text or graphics, enables the reader's eyes to take quick breaks. White space also makes the page look less intimidating. When designing each page, there should be white space in the top, bottom and side margins, between columns, and within the text itself by using subheads and left alignment.

Dummy your layout

It may be helpful to dummy or sketch your layout on paper before producing it on your computer. To do so, make a list of your stories, noting any photo or graphical elements that go with them, and rate the stories by importance. Then, on a piece of paper, sketch where the banner, mast-head, articles, headlines and photos or graphics will be placed. Your most important stories should be placed on page 1.

For a brochure, fold the paper to your brochure's size and follow the same steps.

Creating a dummy of your layout will help you determine if you have enough content for your publication, see where there will be "holes" that need to be filled and see where a graphical element is needed to break up text and make your publication easier to read.

Brochure elements

The same elements of design apply to creating a readable and usable brochure. In essence, a brochure is a small newsletter focused on one topic or message. Either bi-folded or tri-folded, a brochure should include

- a cover page with a headline stating what the brochure is about
- headlines and subheads on the inside pages to break up the text

Proofread your publication

Once your newsletter or brochure is formatted into your template, it is beneficial to have another person proofread it for you. Besides reading through your articles for spelling, grammar, and content clarity, your proofreader should review

- headlines to ensure they accompany the correct stories
- jumps, or continued articles, to ensure they flow correctly
- graphics and photos to ensure they are placed with the correct story and are not distorted in any way
- table of contents to ensure the correct page numbers are listed
- date and issue number of the publication to ensure they are correct
- color for consistency throughout the publication
- font usage and type size for consistency throughout the publication
- remember: always run spell-check.

Tools needed for newsletter design and production

Newsletters are easily created with the help of a computer (either a PC or an Apple Macintosh) and desktop publishing software. Desktop publishing applications such as Microsoft Publisher and Print Shop come with ready-made templates that have the headline and column areas, fonts, type size and colors already defined for you. These are easily customizable for your audience by dropping in your text, headlines and photos or graphics.

Design applications such as Adobe PageMaker and QuarkXPress are widely used in the design world and offer more flexible design options. When using these applications, you will need to create the template yourself.

Most desktop publishing software applications come with tutorials that will take you through the elements of the program and show you how to use it.

Newsletters and brochures can also be laid out using word processing applications such as Microsoft Word or Microsoft Works Word Processor. Keep in mind though, that word processing applications were designed to process words, not manipulate text and graphics on a page.

Having a digital camera or scanner is also beneficial for newsletter design. A digital camera enables you to upload a photograph to your computer. A scanner will scan your image into your computer. When your photograph or image is uploaded or scanned, you will be able to place it into your newsletter using your desktop publishing software.

Send your print publication to press

There are three ways to make copies of your publication for distribution—photocopying, desktop printing, or professional printing.

> **Photocopying:** Consider photocopying your publication if it is letter or legal sized, you need a small quantity and color is not an issue. Note: photographs and shaded areas will be of lesser quality when photocopied.

> **Desktop printing:** Consider using your desktop printer if your publication is letter or legal sized, you need a small quantity and you are concerned about the quality of photographs and shaded areas.

> **Professional printing:** Consider using a professional printer if you need a larger quantity, are using multiple colors, are concerned about the quality of shaded areas or artwork, or are using heavy or textured paper. Note: when using a professional printer, be sure to get bids for your print job. Make a list of your publication's specifications, including number of pages, paper on which it is to be printed, ink colors used, the number of copies and if it is to be folded, stapled or finished in another fashion.

Additional design resources

Visit your local library or bookstore and browse through the many available books about desktop publishing and graphic design. From design basics to detailed information about using type, color or graphics, you are sure to find a resource that fits your needs.

Additionally, the Internet has a wealth of information on desktop publishing and design, including tutorials and online classes.

Chapter 7

Hiring a Communications Consultant

J. Ron Byler

In the more than 25 years I've worked for faith-based organizations, one of the most important things I'm continuing to learn is when to rely on the expertise of a consultant. A consultant can add to your knowledge base, consider important factors you may have otherwise overlooked, give you increased credibility, expand your capacities, build on the experience of others, and provide an outside perspective.

On the other hand, if not chosen carefully, a consultant can increase your workload, give you bad advice based on poor research, provide "cookie cutter" counsel that does not fit your organization, answer questions you were not asking, and respond so late that information learned is no longer relevant.

Simply put, a consultant is someone you rely on for professional or technical advice or opinions. Of course, this happens informally on a regular basis. You and your staff consult with each other regularly. You consult with your peers in your own organization or with those you know in other organizations. But sometimes, you may need a more formal arrangement. Knowing when is the right time to hire a consultant is the first key to hiring one.

"When confronted with a serious problem, our first instinct all too often is to look for some outside guru who can guide us through it," says David Baum in his book, *Lightning in a Bottle: Proven Lessons for Leading Change* (Dearborn Company, 2000). Too often, we consider hiring consultants because we lack the confidence to rely on our own skills and judgments and those of the people we work with on a daily basis.

Occasionally, however, you'll find it's important to get an outside perspective. Or you simply may not have enough "hands" to do the work that needs to be done. Or perhaps you're facing a communications challenge that you or your staff simply have not faced before. Hiring a consultant is one resource to help you get the job done.

Choosing the right consultant

There are many different types of consultants who can assist you in your communications work. I've used consultants to do market research to help me better understand my constituency, to design visual identity programs, to conduct communications audits, to produce video and print resources, to plan public events, to strategize media relations programs, and more.

Some consultants work for consulting or communications firms. Others are experienced professionals who are now working on their own. Still others are staff persons for existing agencies who are looking for additional income or who need new challenges. You can benefit from consulting with each of these types, depending on the kind of work that needs to be done, your capacity to manage the work and your available funding.

Make sure you consider a variety of options available to you. Talk to people who know other people. Look for examples of the kinds of work you need done. Think about the skills and perspectives that are most important for your organization and the task at hand. Interview at least several people who you think might fit your needs.

As you evaluate your options, a good consultant will demonstrate

Understanding of your organization—You are responsible for making sure your consultant understands your faith group or organization. Has the consultant worked for groups like yours before? Does the consultant demonstrate an ability to listen to your unique situation? Is he/she asking the right questions?

Experience and track record from similar assignments—One of the primary reasons you want to consider engaging consultants is because they have experience you don't. What projects have the potential consultants worked on previously that demonstrate their experiences to address your particular situation?

Sensitivity to your values, mission, community and culture—Faith groups and non-profit organizations have different needs and missions than others. Has your prospective consultant worked in your kind of environment before? Does the consultant probe to understand your faith group's perspective on the issue at hand?

Capacity to deliver on time—Check this one out carefully with references! Is the consultant reliable? Is he/she willing to adhere to a schedule? (Of course, you also need to complete your part of the work in a timely fashion as well.) Whether or not a consultant arrives on time for interviews and responds promptly to your requests is probably a good indication of what you will encounter later.

Connections that will work for you—Build a network of people around you who are potential consultants. When you need a consultant, the people you know and trust, the people who have already demonstrated their capabilities, are the ones you will most readily want to engage.

Preparing to hire a consultant

There is work you need to do before you are ready to hire a consultant. Define your objectives and goals. What is the problem you need to solve? What is it you want to accomplish? What information do you already possess? Be as specific as possible in outlining your needs and expected outcomes.

The sidebar, Guidelines for Hiring a Consultant, provides a checklist for preparing to hire a consultant. The more work you do to define your needs before hiring a consultant, the better your chances for success.

As you clarify your expectations, develop a prospectus that outlines the communications problem to be solved. Gather related information that will give your potential consultants adequate background. Think carefully about the authority channels your consultant will need to follow and develop a time line for the project. You will also want to identify the points in the project where you want to be a part of the decision-making process and/or authorize further work.

Guidelines for Hiring a Consultant

Define your goals
Know what your goal is. The more specific you are, the more likely your consultant can help you achieve your objective.

Evaluate alternatives
The more comfortable you are with a consultant, the more productive that relationship will be. Interviewing multiple candidates will help you find the person who is the best match.

Look for experience
One of the main reasons for hiring a consultant is because you need special expertise. Look for someone who can transfer his or her experience from other engagements to your case.

Look for learners
Good consultants constantly learn. They're open-minded and they're intellectually engaged. They're experts, but they're also confident enough to say when they don't know something.

Ask for input
By all means, invite your candidates to share their thoughts about the engagement being discussed. They may even help you redefine your goals.

Ask for a proposal
After you've met with one or several candidates, who you feel could help, ask for written proposals. This is an opportunity for candidates to demonstrate their understanding of your problem and provide a framework for addressing it.

Check references
While references will always speak positively (or else they wouldn't be offered), be sure to find out how the consultant handles unforeseen problems.

Be honest
If something is nagging you about a particular candidate, say what's on your mind. It will clear the air and it's a great way to get a relationship off to a good start.

Used with permission from the Consulting Exchange (www.consultingexchange.com)

Interviewing potential consultants

If possible, plan to interview your consultant candidates on location at your agency. Introduce them to the people with whom they will be working. Allow enough time for informal conversations with other staff members.

The sidebar, Questions to ask a prospective consultant, can guide you in getting to know your potential candidates, determining whether they have the skills you need and deciding which one is the best fit for your particular project. Be sure to allow time in the interview for the candidates to ask you questions as well. Often, their questions will help you clarify your own needs and narrow the focus of work.

Pay special attention to your comfort level, and that of your staff, in interacting with the potential candidates. The success of your project depends on the working relationship and trust level you develop with the consultant, as well as the particular skills they bring to the work.

When you make your hiring decision, you will want to develop a formal contract or an informal memo of agreement outlining your basic understandings about the scope of the project, the deliverables, the payment and the schedule. Be especially clear about the delivery schedule. In my experience, the time line for completing the project is the factor that can most often become a later point of contention.

Another issue you will want to consider is ownership of the material after the project is completed. For example, in a video or print project, will you allow elements to be used by the consultant with other clients? After the project is completed, are you free to use parts of it in other projects not involving the consultant without additional payment? Will the consultant have permission to use parts of your project for promotional purposes or to quote research in articles or news stories?

Questions to ask a prospective consultant

- What strengths do you possess that will prove particularly helpful in connection with this project?

- Have you worked on similar projects or consulted with other groups facing problems similar to ours? What did you learn from the experience? What would you do differently if you could repeat the experience?

- How would you describe the challenges we face from the limited amount you now know about us?

- Describe your work process. How would you work with our staff, board and executive director?

- Are there other members of your consultant team who would be working with you? Who are they? How would you propose to divide up the tasks among your team members? When can we interview them?

- What problems do you anticipate as we begin our work together? How can we best address these problems early on?

- Talk about the responsibilities we must assume in order to make our work together successful.

- Are you available to complete the work during the time we've specified?

- What else should we be asking you? What else should we know about you, your experience or what it would be like to work together?

Used with permission from Consultants Ontap (www.ontap.org).

Completing a successful consultant relationship

The success of your work with consultants depends as much on you as on the consultant you hire. You need to be honest about the problems you face and you need to give your consultant the whole story—even details that may be embarrassing to you or to your faith group or agency. Be ready to respond to your consultant's requests in a timely manner.

You will also want to give your consultant access to your staff and board as needed. Let others know about the work the consultant is doing and why. In the consulting process, you and your staff will also learn new skills that you will be able to apply to future projects and situations.

One of your most difficult assignments after you've hired a consultant is to be ready to follow the consultant's recommendations and advice. Often this advice can mean significant change for you and your organization—change in your agency's image, change in how you understand your constituency, or change in how you do your work. Remember that one of the strengths consultants bring to their work with you is their outside perspective. Be prepared to help your staff and board respond to your consultant's recommendations.

When the consultant's work is completed, be sure to schedule an exit interview. Ask for advice on how the relationship could have been strengthened or how the task could have been focused more clearly. Probe for ways in which the consultant can continue to be available to you, even informally, after the consultant relationship has officially ended.

In short, building strong, trustworthy relationships with your consultants makes more than good business sense. It also demonstrates the foundation of caring and concern your faith-base organization values.

May all of your future consultant relationships bear good fruit!

Chapter 8

Media: Didn't I See You on TV?

By Kermit Netteburg

Radio and television define what is important in our lives. We know the latest American Idol better than our next door neighbors. We wake up in the morning and reach for the remote to check the news on CNN or SportsCenter on ESPN. We put a radio in the shower, and the drive to work goes better when we hear about a traffic jam that may be 20 miles away.

We even know more people who've found romance on dating games than in religious gatherings.

Media define reality. It's called "Agenda Setting." Research tells us that the media don't tell us what to think, but they do tell us what to think about. If we want people to consider religion as an important part of their lives we must have a media presence.

Even small audiences on media create a greater awareness of your religious organization. Consider how big the media audience is. Say your pastor wants his sermons broadcast on a radio station in a major city like Houston. That station probably will reach only 1 or 2 percent of the total audience, and the pastor's sermon may reach less than that. That means more than 98 percent of people won't hear your message. But in a city like Houston that still means 20,000 people or more. Even if your pastor's congregation has 200 people, he won't preach to that many people in two years. (I'm giving the pastor a few weeks vacation each year!) Media are essential if faith groups are to be known in the community.

Media also are essential for reaching people related to your own organization as well. The faithful may miss this week's service at the mosque or synagogue, but they can attend via radio. People may have moved from one city to another, and they may be looking for a faith community similar to the one they left; if they see you on television, they feel more comfortable visiting your house of worship for the first time. Former members may be looking for a way to return to the faith of their childhood; a presence on radio or television may seem more credible.

 So how do faith groups use media to be known in the community and to meet the needs of members? Seven types of programs may be valuable for local faith-based organizations:

Worship services
This is the most common form of religious programming, dominated largely by Christian faiths. It's also the best way to give a window into what your organization is really like, and it's a great way to keep in touch with members who don't attend services on some week.

Special events
A church may join with other community organizations to broadcast a performance of Handel's "Messiah." A mosque may show a program that depicts Ramadan observances. A synagogue may have a special event to celebrate 100 years of service to its members and the community. Any special event that commemorates important facets of the faith is a wonderful time to give the community a chance to see your faith group in action.

Spot announcements and advertisements

Public service announcements were a staple of religious organizations for decades. The Federal Communication Commission has relaxed those requirements, but stations still want to broadcast announcements of local events. Advertising costs more than free announcements, but you also guarantee when it will air—and that it will air!

Talk shows

These programs are simpler to produce than dramas or news documentaries, even easier than worship services. Talk shows on relevant topics are a staple of public-broadcasting channels. Talk radio has become one of the largest formats, with a large number of adult male listeners.

Interview placements on other talk shows

When you place someone as the guest on a talk show, you provide exposure for your faith community without having to create an entire talk show yourself. However, talk show intervie-wees should establish clear goals for the interview.

National programs produced by your faith group

Many faith groups produce national programs from a headquarters office. These can be valuable to place on local radio and television stations.

National spots produced by your faith group

The same thing is true of spot announcements. These short-format spots have helped many religious organizations be viewed more positively.

Broadcasting Your Worship Services

Nothing gives people a clearer view of your faith group than being able to see and/or hear a worship service. Christian churches dominate religious broadcasting, but showing services from other faiths could be equally important. This is especially true of special religious services, including pilgrimages and similar religious events.

Faith groups that wish to broadcast their worship services should answer five questions before planning what to do:

- Why do we want to broadcast the services?
- What is our target audience?
- Do we want to broadcast weekly, or only occasional special events?
- Do we want to broadcast live, or via tape delay?
- Do we want to broadcast a 30- or 60-minute excerpt of the worship service, or the full worship service?

Most Christian churches broadcast their worship services to reach non-members and acquaint them with the church. These churches frequently broadcast their full worship service live each week. This allows members who don't make it to church that week to view the services.

It's probably better to broadcast via tape delay, because it gives increased opportunity to improve the program. Dead air can be removed. Portions of the worship service with poor sound can be improved or eliminated. Tape delay, however, creates its own needs. You have to be sure the service is somewhat timeless. Don't refer to specific events of the past day or week. Special services for Christmas or Yom Kippur will run "after the fact."

 Tips for broadcasting on radio

Worship services often sound wonderful in the church, mosque, or synagogue. However, they may not sound as good on radio. Capturing a choir's music, or capturing congregational singing, requires expertise—and the strategic placement of good quality microphones. If you plan to broadcast the service regularly, get professional help to capture the sound effectively.

People listening on radio can't see your service. You'll need to coach worship leaders to describe actions that are happening. You'll also need to plan worship services that can be understood by the radio audience. This is another reason for tape delay; editing out the "visual" parts of the service makes the service more valuable to the listener.

People listening on radio also don't have bulletins. They need an announcer who tells them what will happen during the service. This "radio host" doesn't need to be part of the worship service, but should open and close the program so that the listener has a sense of completeness. The radio host also makes the worship service more personal.

Faith groups with a history of taping the messages during the worship service may want to consider creating a 30-minute daily worship message. This can be done by editing the messages, creating liners—the beginning and ending for the program—and then packaging this as a program. These are especially useful for airing on religious radio stations, a strong and growing part of the radio industry.

Tips for broadcasting on television

Many of the tips associated with radio apply to television as well. Good sound is essential. A host creates an effective framework for the program. Your worship may be new to many people and it may need explaining.

Television demands good visuals. Very few houses of worship are ready for television without significant remodeling. In virtually every instance, lighting will have to be improved, and you need to ask help from a professional. Likewise, the look of the stage area will need to work on camera. Many wonderful rostrums look terrible on television. Once again, seek the advice of a television designer.

The number and quality of cameras will depend upon your usage. If you want to provide only a closed-circuit telecast to another room because you have overflow crowds, a single camera may be sufficient. A single camera also will suffice if you are televising the service only to an adjoining facility such as a hospital or school.

If the service is to be broadcast or cablecast, you should plan to have at least three cameras, maybe a jib camera, maybe a remote from the back wall.. These don't have to be expensive. Good cameras can be purchased for about $5,000. It's at least as important to have good lighting and a good stage as it is to have good cameras.

Live television is almost never done, even by networks with extremely sophisticated personnel. Faith groups should almost never consider live television if they plan to broadcast on over-the-air stations; instead everything should be prerecorded. This also allows for post production that can make the broadcast even better.

Special Events

These events almost require a separate and special production crew. Your task as the communication leader for your faith community is to create a great program. Let professionals handle the production.

One of the best ways to do this is to partner with other community groups and then ask local television outlets to produce the television broadcast. They may even do it for free.

Cable access channels in many communities also have crews that will help produce on-site events. Check with your cable company.

Spot Announcements and Advertisements

These can be as sophisticated as a Ford commercial and as simple as words on a screen. The more you put into the production of the spots, the greater the likelihood of their being used, watched and remembered!

It's vital to involve a media professional. There may be members of your faith community who work in the media; tap their expertise. They may be camera operators, editors, script writers, or designers. They all know the field, and will be helpful.

If no one in your faith group is a professional, contact a professional agency. The perspective of someone outside your faith group may help you focus your message more clearly.

These professionals will help you understand the tricks of the trade to get a full message conveyed in 30 or 60 seconds. They'll help you learn how to grab a viewer's attention and how to retain it.

If you have an event of community interest, you can contact the local radio or television stations directly. They'll help you put together the announcement for their bulletin board programs. Before you go to see them, get together a fact sheet that tells the nature of the event, who the audience is, when and where it will occur, why it will be valuable to the community, and any other pertinent details. This will help the media determine whether they should produce spots for you.

Finally, your national or international faith group probably has spots that you can adapt to your local setting. Contact them and ask for assistance.

Talk Shows

Talk radio is one of the boom markets. Rush Limbaugh and Dr. Laura have become household names. On television, Larry King and Bill O'Reilly have successful talk shows. While you may not reach that large a market, talk shows can be an important way for you to communicate with the community and establish the purposes of your faith organization.

Talk shows are less expensive to produce than other kinds of programs. They also can target current events, thus helping your church be part of the ongoing dialogue in the community.

Talk shows on radio face a few challenges. One is having quick-witted people on air, because there isn't a script. Another is not having too many people on a talk show. That can confuse the listener who can't figure out which person is talking. Limit your radio talk show to no more than three people.

Talk television is a special challenge. You need to have good visuals. This requires clear pictures of the people who are talking. Don't have distracting plants or backgrounds. Have a table people can gather around. Establish the entire group with a wide shot; use close-ups of people's faces when they are speaking. Talk television will never be as exciting as an adventure movie, but it can be an important way to contribute to community discussions.

Distributing Your Programs

Many people focus on creating programs, and then are bewildered when it comes to getting them on air. Start with a plan in mind for how your program will air.

Local stations

These are often favored by religion communicators, because they already have an audience. That's true, but the audience isn't necessarily ready to listen to your program. Before you visit the television station, have an idea when your program should air in order to meet your needs and their goals. Before you visit the radio station, know what format they use and be ready to explain how your program fits into that format.

Cable television

Cable systems always have a local-access channel for public use. Cable companies have crews to run all the electronic gear that can look pretty intimidating. The systems also generally maintain public-access studios, usually available for free. This can provide you with a location for your talk show.

Cable stations also take prerecorded programs. Check with the cable company to determine what format of videotape they want.

Some communicators don't think very highly of local-cable-access channels. You should understand their value. Their audiences are often small, but their audiences also are those most connected with the community. After all, they're watching the local-cable-access channel because they'd prefer to know about their town instead of some fictitious town on television. So you will be communicating with the thought leaders of the community, the people who care about what's happening in town. That makes cable access channels are very good distribution method.

Webcasting

The World Wide Web can expand your audience well beyond the geography of your local faith community. Webcasting continues to grow, and the quality of the signal continues to improve. I know one proud parent who listens to his son's sermons because they are Webcast. Streaming audio and video can be complemented with archived programs as well.

Duplication

When you've created the audio or video program, it's simple to create CDs and DVDs and cassettes. If one of your goals is to distribute your worship service to people who aren't able to attend, a cassette is wonderful. If another goal is to share copies of your talk programs with community thought leaders, a cassette is a valuable tool (a CD may be more valuable). If you had a special event and want to let other people see it, a DVD or videocassette extends the reach of the program.

This may seem like old technology, but it still communicates with many people. People like to be able to watch or listen at their own convenience; this distribution method accomplishes that.

Evaluating Your Broadcasts

Now you've been on the air for six months or a year. Is the broadcast a good idea? Has it been worth the effort? Is it a wise use of money?

Answering those questions—and others like them—is the reason for research. Faith groups are not likely to get Arbitron or Nielsen data, but there still are ways to evaluate what you've done.

Did you reach your goals?
One of the reasons it's important to know what you want to accomplish is so that you can know if you reached that goal. If you wanted lots of people to visit your faith community, did it happen? If you wanted to break down prejudices about your unknown or misunderstood group, have you experience less prejudice? If you wanted members to take greater pride in your faith group, have people mentioned anything to you?

Review the programs
Bring a group of professionals together to watch several programs. The reviewers don't have to be members of your faith group and it's best if at least some of them aren't. In this evaluation group, have everyone look at the program and ask how it could be made better.

What has been your audience response?
Most faith groups ask for some type of response from their programs. Write in to get a booklet. Call for more information. Donate funds to the program or to some other special cause. Always keep track of the number of requests for information or donations. Then ask if the response is worth the effort and cost of broadcasting the program.

A Final Note

Radio and television are extremely sophisticated media. Many stations and networks produce programs you can't possibly begin to mirror. You don't have the budget of a network television show, and you can't buy the research that creates successful talk radio. But don't be discouraged.

What you can produce are programs that share simple messages about faith. Many people want to hear faith-building and faith-affirming programs. They are your audience. Don't let them down.

Writing for Radio
Radio is a personal medium. People listen to the radio alone. So be friendly. Don't talk to a crowd; talk with a friend.

Radio is a background medium. People listen while they're driving, cooking, working. So be simple. Don't make a lot of complex, complicated ideas. Instead, focus on one thing. In a longer program, focus on one thing at a time.

Radio is an aural medium. People listen to it. They can't back up and read that paragraph again. So make the sentences short, with one idea to a sentence. Repeat important information, and tell people what's coming up next in your program.

Radio can't be cluttered. Simplify everything. Round off numbers. Avoid extraneous information. Follow the KISS principle—Keep It Short and Simple!

Writing for Television

Television is a visual medium. People watch television. So think about what will be seen before you think about what will be said. Religious broadcasters especially tend to create "talking head" programs. Think about how your program will look on television, and how you can make it more visually appealing.

Television is a star-driven medium. People tune in to see their favorite performers. So think about who will be the "star" of your television program. A host of a talk show. A spokesperson for a community program. A preacher for a worship service program. Design the program so the star becomes a personality that people want to see and hear.

Television is a remote-control medium. The viewer has a remote in her hand; she will use it. Every moment of the program has to be enticing. Something new needs to happen on the screen at least every 10 seconds, preferably more often.

Television is watched alone, or in small groups. Be personal. Talk with a friend, don't shout to an arena.

Chapter 9

Surfing Your Faith Community:
Building a Presence on the World Wide Web

by Jeanean D. Merkel

If You Build It They Will Come

Recently I helped set up a computer for a friend's parents. His 82-year-old mother wanted it for her 88-year-old husband, so that he could play cards now that his social circles were dwindling. It was only during the set up and installation of the card-game software that my friend's mother began to realize how much more the computer could do when connected to the Internet. They could send and receive e-mail with children and grandchildren, get news from their hometown, and research health concerns.

Her first e-mail read: "I want to know what a URL is."

Another Web surfer was born. And this great-grandmother, who never dreamed she would be using a computer, has found new insights and information relevant to her life. She's certainly not alone. The Pew Internet Project estimates that more than one-fifth of Internet users (19-20 million people) have sought spiritual and religious information on the Internet.[1]

A Barna Research Group study found that 8 percent of adults and 12 percent of teenagers use the Internet for religious or spiritual experiences. George Barna, who directed the study, anticipates that "By the end of the decade [2010] we will have in excess of 10 percent of our population who rely upon the Internet for their entire spiritual experience. Some of them will be individuals who have not had a connection with a faith community, but millions of others will be people who drop out of the physical church in favor of the cyberchurch."[2]

Introduction

We're now more likely to send an e-mail than a letter, to research a topic online rather than in an encyclopedia, to check directions on Mapquest rather than in an atlas. We can't escape the Internet and we can't ignore it, so how can faith communities harness this cultural revolution to extend their ministries? For most, it means having an Internet presence, a Web site, because when almost 200 million Americans look for information, inspiration, and resources on the Web, if they don't find you, they'll find someone else who does meet their needs.

See CD for glossary of terms.

Four-steps to an online presence

A Web site is one element of an organization's communication program. But, it's a distinctive, on-demand production: part brochure, part voice mail, part video, part phone book. This chapter is intended to help you develop a Web site that is relevant, relational, and realistic. If you have an existing Web site, these steps help you align your site more closely with your organization's needs and mission.

Because a Web site is a communication tool (along with your newsletter, brochures, signs, and events), a successful site follows the basic communications model:

- Research
- Plan
- Execute
- Evaluate

Step One: Research

Here are six questions to answer before initiating a Web site:

1. What is the purpose of your Web site?

Ask yourself: Why do we need a Web site? "Everyone else has one" isn't good enough. What, specifically, do you want it to do for your publics? For example, listing the times of regular services may reduce the number of phone calls. In another case, you might place two minutes of a videotaped program on the site to provide information.

2. How does your site serve your goals?

A Web site can use a variety of media. It can take the best of your existing print, graphic, and audio materials. It is also capable of enabling two-way communication in new ways (feedback, discussion boards, and forums). Once you learn what the Web does well, you can match those capabilities to your organization's mission and your communication goals.

3. Who is the audience?

While you may have one particular audience in mind—your adherents, those who attend services or your donors—the World Wide Web is a public forum. That means everyone will be able to access your Web site unless you password-protect it. Keep this public interest aspect in mind as you plan.

You may be tempted to say your site is for everyone, but you need to define your various audiences. For instance, the audience for a Web site for a house of worship could include registered adults, children in education programs, and members of volunteer groups.

If you're seeking to expand your mission and ministry into the community, how will you tell people your site is there? You may need to revise advertising, stationery, brochures, and other printed materials to include your site's address.

4. How will you measure success?

Establish goals that are measurable and specific to your situation. Here are some samples:

- Reduce the number of calls to the office by 25 percent in one year.

- Increase donations by 5 percent within one year through online giving.

- Reduce the number of printed and mailed newsletters by 20 percent within two years by moving readers to the online version.

5. How will you keep it fresh?

Just as a publication, a radio show or a television production, a Web site is a living organism. Plan for new "editions" of your Web site by identifying material that needs to be changed daily, weekly, monthly, quarterly, and annually.

You also need to consider the resources necessary to keep the site fresh. Who will create the content? Who will put it into the site? Who will determine when it changes? If you're using current staff, figure out what current tasks can be modified so that they can handle the additional work required for site maintenance. If you have only non-technical staff, provide content management software that allows users to organize and make changes to a Web site through a word-processor-like interface. Typically these users do not need to know HTML.

6. Who are your stakeholders?

The more people who are involved at the outset, the fewer headaches you'll have later on. Get input from any internal group that will use or update the site. Include some of your key publics in a planning group for input and feedback as the development moves forward. Include decision makers on your team so that the group doesn't stall or get bogged down. Make clear who will make the decisions. And, finally, involve those who will build the site—they'll have important elements for you to consider as you move forward.

Step 2: Plan

Set a timeline for your Web site project. This not only will help you reach the finish line, but also will help determine the scope of your project.

A short timeline means few bells and whistles. That may be fine for special events or other time-limited sites. Even so, you'll need to find someone who can produce it within your timeframe.

If time is no object, let the scope and content determine your timeline so that you can:

- Develop a creative presentation.
- Take photos and add design graphics that support your theme and content.
- Write or commission someone to provide the content.

Begin concrete planning:

- Ask everyone what should be included.
- Evaluate all the suggestions and delete those that aren't relevant to your mission and goals.
- Organize all the relevant material into a "site map."

Site maps that look like organization charts work well at this point. Your site's home page is the starting point. From there, the elements will depend on what you're trying to achieve. For a synagogue, church, or temple, for instance, you might have sections called: About Us, Calendar, Ministries, and Education. "About Us" pages might include a welcome message, a schedule of services, directions, staff listing, and contact information.

Once you've decided what your categories and their sub-pages will be, the next step is to plan how you will develop the content. Writing for the Web could be its own topic in this handbook, but the important points are:

Make it brief.

Include links.

Provide bullet items to make copy visually interesting and to make it readable at a glance.

Add a reasonable number of graphics to enhance the page.

 You will also need to collect graphics, photos (and permissions to use them). At our organization, we've found that a storyboard helps us be consistent, complete, and allows us to easily correct text as it's developed.

Questions for reflection when building a Web site:

1. What makes the Internet a key tool?

Gets your message directly to the publics you serve.

Has a potential audience size that exceeds the reach of other media/communication tools.

Is a powerful tool combining visual and print messages.

Allows for interactivity.

2. How do you make the Internet work for you?

Create a visually compelling site.

Tell a story.

Use simple, intuitive navigation tools.

Invite your visitors to communicate with you.

3. What do you need to consider before you start?

Who are you? (an in-depth analysis of your messages).

How do your members/publics perceive you now?

How do you wish to tell your story?

Who is your audience and what do they want to know?

What are your resources for Web site creation and maintenance?

Who can help you in development?

Step 3: Execute

Here are tips to bring your Web site together:

1. Select a theme derived from a logo or slogan. This can help give the site coherence and offer hints for the "voice" you want the site to have (official, friendly, or casual).

2. Find a Web-friendly color scheme. There are 216 "browser-safe" colors. These are colors that will display in the same hues and tone on all browsers, ensuring that your design will be consistent for most of your visitors. Find a combination that is pleasing to you and will be of interest to your viewers.

 3. Use templates. If you plan your pages using a template and style sheet, you will have a coherent site rather than one in which individual pages look as if each came from a different book. Coherence comes from consistency in typeface, alignment, color, and layout. Templates also allow you to easily change the overall look of your site.

 4. Vary templates for depth and interest. You want consistency, but you don't want every page to look exactly the same. You need to provide variations on the template to keep things interesting for your visitors and to provide a stamp of individuality for independent sections.

5. Adapt graphic-design skills. Just because you're on the Web, don't ignore graphic design basics. While photo resolution is lower on the Web than in print (usually about 72 dots per inch), you can apply elements like collages, shadows for photos, and color to indicate navigation elements.

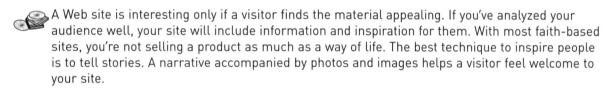 A Web site is interesting only if a visitor finds the material appealing. If you've analyzed your audience well, your site will include information and inspiration for them. With most faith-based sites, you're not selling a product as much as a way of life. The best technique to inspire people is to tell stories. A narrative accompanied by photos and images helps a visitor feel welcome to your site.

 Interactive elements also draw people to Web sites. You might consider offering prayers, ways for people to send prayer requests, discussion boards on topics of interest, photo galleries, donation forms, invitations to events, and registration forms.

Be wary of "bright shiny objects." Many features are available and it's tempting to use them all—blinking text, music, Flash®, and animated gifs like the mailbox that opens and closes endlessly. Limit the number of special effects not only because they aren't relevant, but also because they may cause people to leave the site. Animations and large graphics also take a long time to load. Sometimes a designer with a high-speed line forgets that most users have a dial-up connection with speeds 95 percent slower.

A study by Miller and Schneiderman shows that Web users rate good download times at up to five seconds; average download time as six to10 seconds and poor download time as anything over 10 seconds. The moral: Design so you're better than average.

Although more people switch to high-speed connections every day, close to 70 percent of Web users browse with a 56K modem with a connection speed around 45K, versus 1,000K or more for DSL or cable modem. Half your site's visitors—and maybe more—will view your site through a dial-up connection. (Broadband access is increasing rapidly.)

You can't do it all yourself. At some point you will need to engage Web professionals to help you. You can turn to graphic designers, HTML programmers, editors and/or proofreaders, and Internet technology experts including a server provider. A key resource is your hosting service—the business that stores your site on a server and provides your technical support.

Ready for the launch?

First, test, test, and test again to make sure forms, e-mail forwarding, and internal links are working. Copyedit to be sure all contact information, facts and figures are correct. Make sure your server is ready and your domain is active. If you have a new domain name, you may have to allow several days between registration and the recognition of your site by the Internet's domain name servers—the Web's phone directory. Finally, register the site with the major search engines (Google, Yahoo, and Lycos).

Announce your new site to your constituents. To create excitement, have a launch party and invite key publics to react to the new site. Host an open house that includes a preview area. You might also send a news release to area newspapers if your site is of broad interest. Put your domain name and e-mail address on every printed piece you have and create links from related sites such as faithandvalues.com. In addition, if you have any association with institutions, such as colleges or universities, make sure you're linked from those.

Step 4: Evaluate

The evaluation process begins as soon as the site goes "live." We hear from clients, congregants, donors, friends, and foes about what is right as well as what is wrong. Collecting these thoughts and ideas can be helpful for future development.

If you set measurable goals in Step 1, you'll have a place to start as data comes in. Have calls to your main office decreased? Have donations increased? Have you been able to reduce the number of printed and mailed newsletters?

Schedule a review in six months and in a year to:

- Look at detailed user reports of Web site activity (you should be able to get these from your hosting service).
- Analyze data based on the measurements you set at the outset.
- Consider "user" responses and comments both from inside your organization and outside.
- Evaluate whether your maintenance schedule is working and what pages of the site need updating.

You've entered the brave new world of the Web. Enjoy yourself and know that your efforts are adding support and inspiration to the lives of many.

What gets counted, counts

One way to measure the effectiveness of your Web site is to track who visits what part of the site. Your hosting company should have a program that gives you detailed data about site visitors: where they came from, how they found you (for example, by checking a search engine), and what they did once they arrived.

The example on the next page lists Web pages of a site, starting with the most heavily accessed. In the "Item" column, clicking "Referrers" would show the site from which visitors came – the "referring site."

Rank	Item	Accesses	%	Bytes	%	Visits	%	% of Downloads Successful
1	**Welcome to Busted Halo** /index2.htm [Referrers] [Components]	77,963	1.26	1,544,058,478	4.20	63,190	1.32	75.80
2	**Welcome to Busted Halo.com** / [Referrers] [Components]	68,190	1.11	146,354,389	0.40	54,863	1.15	96.77
3	/fresh.html [Referrers]	64,279	1.04	24,051,140	0.07	54,390	1.14	98.99
4	/cgi-bin/dcforum/dcboard.cgi [Referrers]	27,104	0.44	482,572,935	1.31	18,345	0.38	96.22
5	**Recent Features** /recent.htm [Referrers]	20,276	0.33	48,775,836	0.13	16,990	0.35	97.92
6	**BustedHalo.com/Faith Guides** /faith_guides/guides.htm [Referrers] [Components]	15,551	0.25	247,888,664	0.67	12,934	0.27	92.15
7	/spirituality/spaces.htm [Referrers] [Components]	7,986	0.13	105,601,140	0.29	7,301	0.15	91.36
8	/connections/church_search.htm [Referrers] [Components]	7,845	0.13	500,796,322	1.36	7,111	0.15	93.94
9	/spirituality [Referrers] [Components]	6,681	0.11	28,557,167	0.08	4,609	0.10	28.21
10	**Index of /dimensions** /dimensions [Referrers] [Components]	6,678	0.11	10,808,639	0.03	4,580	0.10	37.16
11	**BustedHalo.com/Question Box** /faith_guides/question_box.htm [Referrers] [Components]	6,374	0.10	72,742,105	0.20	5,500	0.11	97.04
12	**BustedHalo.com/Bible Boot Camp** /faith_guides/boot.htm [Referrers] [Components]	6,298	0.10	133,087,168	0.36	5,644	0.12	91.36

Also of interest is the fact that of the top 12 pages listed, 10 are items available as menu items on the home page.

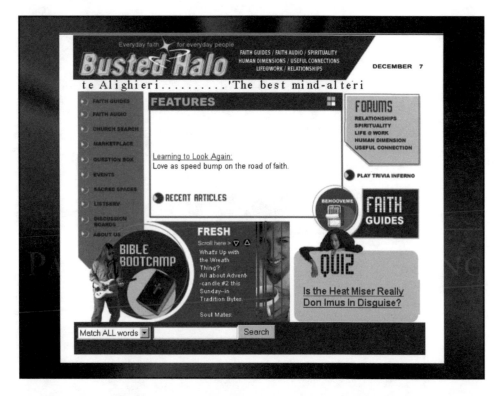

Here's an example of an organization-chart site map, based on an actual site for the Carmelite religious order. Each block or line represents a Web page. This site map shows 54 pages in all.

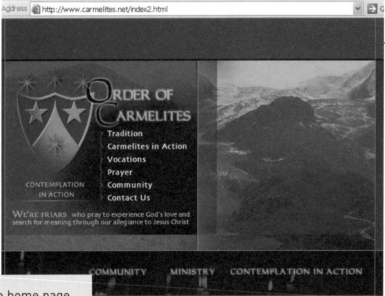

The example above is the home page for www.carmelites.net and corresponds to the first box on the site map. The links to the six main pages appear as text under the title "Order of Carmelites."

The initial page for Carmelites in Action has an introduction and a link to Diversity of Missions and Ministries.

The example above corresponds to the box "Carmelites in Action" on the site map.

The Mission and Ministry page contains an overview and links to five different types of ministry.

The example above corresponds to the box "Diversity of Missions and Ministries" on the site map.

From the home pages, the site has direct links to pages for Tradition, Carmelites in Action, Vocations, Prayer, Community, and Contacts.

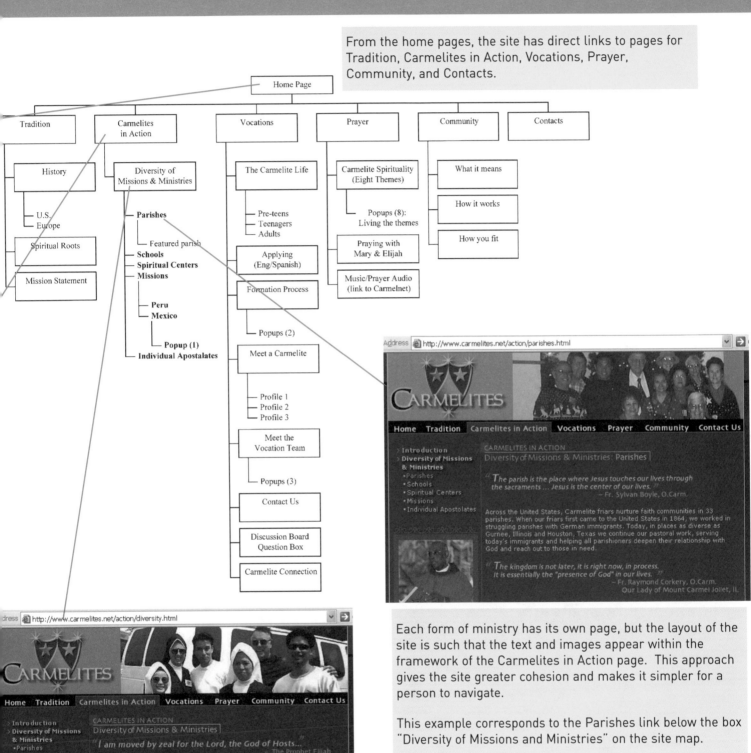

Each form of ministry has its own page, but the layout of the site is such that the text and images appear within the framework of the Carmelites in Action page. This approach gives the site greater cohesion and makes it simpler for a person to navigate.

This example corresponds to the Parishes link below the box "Diversity of Missions and Ministries" on the site map.

1 "Wired Churches, Wired Temples: Taking Congregation and Missions into Cyberspace," December 20, 2001, Pew Internet & American Life Project, Washington, DC.

2 "More Americans Are Seeking Net-Based Faith Experiences," May 21,2001, Barna Research Online, www.barna.org.

Chapter 10

Electronic Presentations:
Not the Same Old Song and Dance

By Rose Pacatte, F.S.P.

Introduction

Journalists know that the key questions to be answered for any story are: who, what, when, where, how, why, and sometimes, how much? These same questions will guide anyone who wants to use one of the best and most simple software presentation techniques available to contemporary communicators: PowerPoint®.

The purpose of PowerPoint (and similar software presentation programs) is to communicate information or to conduct workshops in a logical, well-defined manner, with a beginning, middle, and an end. Some presentation programs are designed to be used specifically within worship services (such as display rolling of lyrics). This chapter, however, will focus on PowerPoint as a communication tool.

If you already know the latest version of Word, you can plunge right into creating a PowerPoint presentation. Follow the prompts of the PowerPoint program. You can design from scratch using a blank template or you can select from a design template and use the AutoContent Wizard to help you build your presentation. Just remember to save your work every few moments and be prepared to spend a few hours practicing.

If you do not know Word or another word processing program, you will not be able to learn PowerPoint on your own without losing years of your spiritual life no matter how hard you try. You will need to take a class or two to learn the basic word processing tools.

Other software presentation programs:

www.seriousmagic.com/presentation.cfm
to create video presentations for PowerPoint

www.tekdeal.com
Corel Presentations using Word Perfect

www.lotus.com
Lotus Freelance and Word Pro

www.openoffice.com
Linux initiative

www.pictures-soft.com
Free alternative software presentation downloads

www.effective-presentation-skills.com
Information and links

www.mindexsoft.com
Slide show Player and Producer

www.KeynotePro.com
(and Themes) from Apple for Mac

www.easyworship.com
EasyWorship for churches

www.mediashout.com
Media Shout worship & presentation software

www.hyperstudio.com
Easy to learn presentation program

www.google.com and search for "presentation tools"

Why PowerPoint? Pro's and Con's

Pro

1. We live in a visual society

   People are used to visuals. Visuals, if prepared well, can hold the attention of the audience of any size longer.

   Boredom is one of the sins in our communication culture today, no matter how precious we perceive our message to be. Visuals can help avoid boredom and loss of attention.

   Visuals appeal to the whole person, not just the cognitive level. They offer a better chance at connecting on an emotional level as well as an intellectual one.

2. We learn and remember more when we can hear and see what is being presented.

3. Visuals can introduce, present and reinforce the message in ways that mere talking cannot do.

4. PowerPoint presentations can generate wonderful handouts for the audience or workshop participants.

5. PowerPoint can produce transparencies for use with an overhead projector in case more updated technical equipment is not available.

Con

1. PowerPoint presentations can become tiresome and even a cliché if not prepared and used well.

2. PowerPoint presentations take practice.

3. The necessary equipment to use PowerPoint fully is costly. Equipment needs include: a LCD projector (digital, multimedia data projector) to project the PowerPoint presentation; a screen (or projection surface); perhaps an auxiliary sound system if the LCD projector's sound reach is limited; and extension cords (See check list at right).

4. The equipment and the environment (lighting, location, acoustics, etc.) may not be adequate. You may also need an experienced assistant to help you set up and be available to adjust equipment as you learn this new song and dance.

Ten ways to use PowerPoint Presentations

1. Workshops and seminars
2. Teaching
3. Meetings
4. Reports
5. Planning Process
6. Worship services
7. Prayer and retreats
8. Wakes and funerals
9. Concerts
10. Clarify thinking

Equipment Checklist for Your PowerPoint Presentation

(If you have an integrated presentation console, you won't need this list)

___ Access to an electrical outlet

___ Laptop computer

___ LCD projector

___ PC or Mac cable to connect the computer and the projector (the PC and Mac cables are different)

___ Screen

___ Power strip

___ Outlet adapter

___ Extension cord

PowerPoint Presentations with Video/DVD

___ Sound check (If you have a DVD player in your computer already, then make sure your sound is loud enough for all to hear; you may have to add an auxiliary sound connection)

___ RCA cables to connect the LCD projector to the video or DVD player

___ Proper cables to connect the LCD projector to a sound system if needed

PowerPoint with an Overhead Projector

___ Print out the presentation one slide at a time on paper and photocopy onto the transparencies or print directly on the transparencies.

Beginners 101 – Basic Training

I have taught basic PowerPoint to church communicators on several occasions. I have the found the following observations and suggestions helpful:

1. If you are in a hurry to learn PowerPoint and don't already know Word, take a class at your local CompUSA (6 hours, as of this writing, was under $200) to learn basic skills. Follow this up with another course on basic PowerPoint if you want to become proficient quickly. If you have more time, perhaps someone in your congregation can tutor you or you can teach yourself.

2. Buy a copy of *Media Ministry Made Easy: a Practical Guide to Visual Communication* by Tim Eason (Abingdon Press, 2003). There is no better resource for faith communities. It comes with a training DVD that will help you to create effective PowerPoint presentations that develop your core concept(s) from the most simple to those that include audio and video.

Beginners 201 – Planning

PowerPoint provides many templates to help you plan and create almost any presentation: Blank Template, Design Template, and the AutoContent Wizard prompt you at every point to develop a presentation. Using these templates for practice will teach you discipline – you will have to articulate exactly what it is you want to communicate visually (color, layout, design, font style, and size) and verbally (key words).

These templates enable presenters to 1) to focus and be specific and 2) finish on time. They empower the audience 1) to pay attention, 2) to learn, 3) to engage in the process and 4) to depart with a sense of fulfillment, having spent their time well.

Sample Outline

To the right is an outline to navigate this discussion:

You need to start with a reason for your presentation. State your objective(s) at the outset. A logical development of the topic, anecdotes to illustrate points, a conclusion, a summary and action items follow in sequence. Sound effects can be added. Music and film clips to present or reinforce a point or start a conversation can be inserted at any time (this takes some technical proficiency) or you can alternate between PowerPoint and the DVD or video source.

Should you prepare a handout?

I think it is a sign of respect for the audience when a PowerPoint handout is made available at the beginning of an interactive workshop session. PowerPoint lets you choose between handouts with one to six frames per page. I prefer the three framed version:

The handouts enable people to know the essentials of your presentation so they can interact freely with you and jot notes as they wish.

Some presenters prefer to give out handouts at the door on the way out. I think it depends on your objectives and your personal style. A handout, which some people may copy, provides the strongest chance for your message to be remembered.

The Blessings of PowerPoint:
Discipline of Structure

Title

Introduction

✍Identify yourself
✍State the purpose of the discussion
✍State the objective(s)

Topics of Discussion

✍State the main ideas you'll be talking about to reach the objective(s)
✍If the presentation is interactive with the audience, tell them what expect them to do

Topic One

✍Details about this topic
✍Supporting information and examples
✍How they relate to your objectives
✍How they relate to your audience

Topic Two

✍Details about this topic
✍Supporting information and examples
✍How they relate to your objectives
✍How they relates to your audience

Topic Three

✍Details about this topic
✍Supporting information and examples
✍How they relate to your objectives
✍How they relate to your audience

The PowerPoint presentation outline uses bullet points, and so should you. Complete sentences are not required. Rambling becomes a thing of the past. Do not read the PowerPoint–talk it. People can see it as you speak. As you learn PowerPoint you will see how you can add comments at the bottom of each slide to prompt you. These will appear on your laptop or computer screen for your eyes only.

PowerPoint is the dream come true for famed speech meister Dale Carnegie, you, the presenter, and the audience.

When PowerPoint is done well, your listeners have something tangible to take away with them, from a spiritual insight to ways to trim the budget.

Remember:

- What objectives do you want to achieve through this presentation?

- How do you propose to achieve them through this presentation?

- What message or information do you want your listeners to know by the end?

Intermediate

By this time you know the following:
- Word (or another word processing program)

- How to plan and create a basic presentation using one or more PowerPoint templates (or other presentation software)

- Whether to provide a handout or not

- Discipline to focus on the who, what, when, where, how and why

- To speak to bullet points and retire your rambling (or preachy) ways forever.

Now you are ready to add art, sound, movement elements to each slide to your presentation. You may have learned some of these techniques from your beginner's class. Once I learned the basics, I learned everything else from others as I watched them prepare PowerPoint presentations and from a conference one-hour workshop.

Do:

- Use the right button on your mouse when creating a PowerPoint presentation or any program. Type a word. Now, highlight the word, click the right side of the mouse on it. Look at the options available to you!

- Now, insert an image from the clip art library in your program and do the same thing. You can format the picture so that it stays where you put it on the page (for example, the text can flow around it.) You can even change the colors of objects and words. You can animate the clip art and the words.

- Keep your sense of humor no matter what happens.

- Practice so you won't panic when (not if) something doesn't work.

- Arrive early to make sure that you have the electrical equipment you will need and that everything is functioning. Be prepared to work off of your handout in case the lights go out. Be cool. It's not the end of the world.

- Remember that how you communicate is what you communicate: "the medium is the message." (Marshall McLuhan)

 Don't:

- Overuse the sound and animation techniques. Too much of a good thing can make the audience lose interest.

- Get flustered if the equipment does not work; switch to your handout.

- Read the PowerPoint presentation; people are watching the slide and listening to you; they get it.

Advanced Attitude 3.0

You are now ready to add a video that complements your presentation.

None of the training courses at CompUSA (www.compusa.com/training/default.asp) teach the user how to include video. So I did a www.google.com search and typed in "how to add video to PowerPoint". One of the results was this site: www.uclaphoto.ucla.edu/How-To's/vidtoppt.htm. Voila'!

However, I didn't have time to learn this. So, I added a DVD drive to my lap top and now I toggle back and forth between the Media Player program and PowerPoint. It's like coordinating a song and dance. It works because I practiced.

Once you know Word (or any word processing program), PowerPoint (or any presentation program) and can search on the Internet, you will become technologically competent, because you are a life-long learner. What a blessing!

Know Your Message and Your Audience

When it comes to PowerPoint, it is necessary to take into account the complexity of your message and the age and physical limitations of your audience.

If the group is under age 35 you can add all the PowerPoint bells and whistles you want. You can add music, visuals and sound effects. But if you are talking fast, and the visuals and sound effects are too fast, you may lose part of your audience. Test your presentation on one or two people from the age group you are addressing and make adjustments.

No matter the age of the group, the way the message is delivered needs to reflect the nature of that message. For example, dancing cartoon figures may not be appropriate for a financial presentation unless the news is very good or you have enough confidence to integrate humor and retain the good will of your audience. You can scan in photographs from a recent church trip and integrate music to create a contemplative prayer service. You can also switch between PowerPoint and video or DVD if you have the proper equipment.

If the group is middle-aged or older, keep the movement of the visuals, and sound effects, to a minimum. Less is more. Persons in this age group are either not used to visual "language" or their eyes and ears cannot keep up. I have MS and I have vision movement problems. I can attest to the fact that I "check out" when I am subjected to a PowerPoint by someone who just learned how cool it is. Just take it down a notch, please.

What about children? I have not yet used PowerPoint with young children. I would suspect that less is more—few slides and few words on those slides, add music and animated clip art. Test it and see.

Lifelong Learning & Evaluations

One way to conduct an evaluation on your presentation is to list the following questions on the last frame of your PowerPoint and the handout:

- What did you like about this presentation?
- What did you learn?
- What would you have preferred to be different?

Show this frame at the end of your presentation. List your e-mail address and ask them to share their thoughts with you. These kinds of questions are more constructive that ranking elements of the presentation from 1 to 5 – which can be devastating.

Peer review is also helpful as is watching how others do their PowerPoints.

Conclusion

I was once stationed at a convent in New York. One young nun there showed so much talent in graphic design that she was asked to begin studying this subject. She already had been published and had an impressive portfolio. One day after she started classes, she said to me, "I know all this stuff. I feel like I am wasting time." I answered her, the way some wise person had once told me, "First learn the rules, then you can creatively break them. Otherwise, you'll never know what you are doing or are capable of."

PowerPoint is a creative tool for communication in a visual culture. Learn the basics and then you can create something wonderful for God and those whom you serve.

Many thanks to: Sister Edward Marie Smith of the Daughters of St. Paul who gave me the courage to learn PowerPoint in the first place; Sister Judith Dieterle, SSL of the Archdiocese of Chicago who gave me many ideas for this chapter and my first formal training in PowerPoint during an hour-long workshop at a religious education conference.

---

* For the purposes of this chapter, I will use Microsoft's PowerPoint and Word programs as my point of reference but you may substitute TekDeal's Corel Presentations that uses WordPerfect (www.TekDeal.com) or any other software bundle that uses a combines a presentation program with a word processing program, often called an "office suite." The consensus is that PowerPoint is the best and most user-friendly for PCs (personal computers/IBM operating systems) rather than Apple (Mac operating system).

Sister Mary Alba's Funeral

A month after 9/11, an older sister of our convent community in Staten Island, NY died suddenly. Sr. Mary Alba had lived on Staten Island on and off for thirty years and was well known and loved. She had lost a dear friend in the World Trade Center tragedy and Sister M. Alba's heart just gave out.

A creative member of our community, Sr. Donna, scanned several photographs of Sr. Mary Alba into the computer and created a two-minute PowerPoint presentation about her life that needed no words.

The wake was held in Our Lady of Pity Church. So in the vestibule of the church Sister Donna set up the laptop computer and a screen, hooked an LCD projector to the computer and set the PowerPoint to "loop continuously."

As visitors entered the church all afternoon and evening, they stopped, signed the memory book, and viewed the brief ongoing slide program: the picture of a woman's life spoke louder than words.

Chapter 11

Other Electronic Tools of Communication

by Bill Southern

Alexander Graham Bell stated his approach to invention and life this way:

> **Leave the beaten track occasionally and dive into the woods. Every time you do so you will be certain to find something that you have never seen before. Follow it up, explore all around it, and before you know it, you will have something worth thinking about to occupy your mind. All really big discoveries are the results of thought.**

Bell's willingness to search out the path less taken resulted in some of the world's most important inventions. It has been said that Bell invented the telephone by searching for it in places where other inventors would never think to look. Bell's ability to believe in the impossible has served the world well.

Sunday, June 25, 1876, was the day of the Battle of the Little Big Horn, or Custer's Last Stand. Far away, in Philadelphia, it was also the day when Bell demonstrated his new invention at the Centennial Exhibition. The exhibition was organized to celebrate the 100th anniversary of the signing of the Declaration of Independence. The telephone was its star attraction.

Alexander Graham Bell knew the importance of his new discovery, not just the impact it would have on the entire world. Bell wrote to his father: "The day is coming when telegraph wires will be laid on to houses just like water or gas—and friends will converse with each other without leaving home." For Alexander Graham Bell, it was the first of many glimpses into the future.

Another great mentor of this author, Albert Einstein, wrote, "Imagination is more important than knowledge." Please use the following information to merely spark your imagination to expand beyond the "9 dots" (your paradigms) and get outside the "box." A "paradigm shift" may be necessary to use available tools in expanding your imagination.

Telephones and Their Uses

Since 1876, the invention of the telephone has undergone hundreds of enhancements. As religious communicators, we should avail ourselves of all avenues of communication.

Possible uses of the telephone beyond the obvious might include:

Phone trees

Fax trees

Phone and fax trees are a great way to spread the word quickly. No one has to make more than a few phone calls, and they're usually calling someone they know—or will get to know over time. Phone trees make communicating easy for large and small organizations.

Telephone Tree

Organizing Committee	Key Contacts	Local Contacts
	a. _____	1. _____ 2. _____ 3. _____ 4. _____
	b. _____	5. _____ 6. _____ 7. _____ 8. _____
A. _____	c. _____	9. _____ 10. _____ 11. _____ 12 _____
	d. _____	13. _____ 14. _____ 15. _____ 16. _____
	a. _____	1. _____ 2. _____ 3. _____ 4. _____
	b. _____	5. _____ 6. _____ 7. _____ 8. _____
B. _____	c. _____	9. _____ 10. _____ 11. _____ 12 _____
	d. _____	13. _____ 14. _____ 15. _____ 16. _____

Your canvass network, based on the 1-in-10 communicators model, has many of the building blocks of a good phone tree—contact information, people communicating with each other, and a good workplace map. Canvassers have a great opportunity to gather phone numbers and recruit volunteers to help work the phone tree. Canvassers will find the phone tree useful as one form of follow-up and ongoing contact with the people they have signed up to telephone.

Here are a few tips for successful Phone Tree operation:

- Try to avoid giving too many calls to any person, and avoid more than two or three levels of contact. This will prevent breakdowns and limit the chance that a message gets confused.

- Provide a script that includes basic information—a meeting, emergency, or prayer request, as well as some background and a contact for more details.

- When possible, build in a back-up system. Ideas include designating "backups" who can take over the calling if needed, ensuring that at least two different people are called within each work area, and have initial callers at the end of the list as well, so they can make sure the message got out.

- Follow-up is critical to the maintenance of an effective phone/fax tree. Callers should report broken 'links' immediately, so that the phone-tree coordinator can track down a new phone number or contact information.

- Test the tree before it's put into operation. Have the phone-tree coordinator double-check the numbers of key contacts, and as many local contacts as possible.

- Phone trees should be checked and updated at least twice each year and then redistributed.

- Phone trees must be kept confidential.

Automated Voice Phone Trees

Several automated devices are now available. The following are a few options for your consideration. (The author does not recommend any of the following. This is only a list for your information and personal investigation.)

VoxAssistant (VPA) functions as a virtual personal assistant that permits remote access and management of communication modes such as e-mail, voicemails, schedules, and calendars. This is done in a manner that the end user wishes to use and is intended to serve as an automated means to accomplish personal and business information management that is otherwise segmented and inefficient for the mobile professional end user.

VoxAlert generates actionable phone alerts based on scheduled events. Users have the option to set alerts for a given date and time. The user can create a message that the system provides as part of the alert condition.

VoxDialer enables callers to place calls using simple voice commands. Callers no longer have to fumble through an address book. The system is connected to the users contact list, which allows the name and number to be utilized for the desired feature.

VoxMail gives the power to access and manage the POP3 Internet access through any working telephone on the planet—no laptops, modems, PDA's enabled phones, or other expensive and clumsy gear required.

PhoneTree Auto Dialer and Emergency Notification System serves any growing organizations that need power and flexibility for both auto dialer message delivery and emergency notification.

These are only a few of the innovations that are available. Use your imagination and get outside the box.

Cell Phones and Their Uses

Alexander Graham Bell probably did not imagine that telephones could be used without lines and cables; however, he would be proud.

Cellular phones have quickly become the telephone of choice for thousands of Americans. Writing in *Life Styles and Past Times*, Jenny Tesar reports, "The latest study from Scarborough Research, the nation's leader in local, regional and national consumer information, shows a 29 percent growth rate for cell phone ownership over the past two years with almost two-thirds (62 percent) of American adults owning a cell phone. In 1984 only 40,000 people used cell phones comparing to the present year 2002, during which 180 million used this device."

They have even become the home telephone, meaning the only phone that some people own. For thousands of people the only method of communication is the cell phone.

Care should be given when calling people on their cell phones due to the cost of some plans that limit the number of minutes available and the additional costs that can be incurred for extra minutes used above the basic allotment. Remember, telephones are for the use of the owner and do not be offended if voice mail is what you receive instead of the person you were calling. Use of voice mail can be extremely beneficial if the caller will leave detailed messages giving the recipient the full reason for the call. The caller can then be given the information they desire on the returned call.

When used properly, the cell phone can be an effective tool in reaching people via phone trees without breaking the chain.

With the expansion of the Internet and cellular phones, text messages, Web browsing and e-mails are now common via cell phones. Cell phones can even be used to send and receive faxes.

Extend the Desktop to Your Mobile Device:

Prepaid Cell Phones: the convenience of no monthly bills and no credit checks for sign up.

Cell Phone Accessories: personalize your phone to make it uniquely yours.

Cell Phone Ringtones: make your phone ring with a melody you choose.

Cell Phone Games: catch the newest wave to take the nation by storm. Cell phone games are games that you can play right on your phone.

Cell Phone Apps: run popular software applications to make your day more productive.

Bluetooth Phones: connect to the World Wide Web through your PDA.

Wifi Phones: home networking protocols built into your phone.

Flash Memory Cards: transfer photos, files and games from your phone to another device.

Eight Rules of Etiquette for Cellular Phone Users

Safety: Pay attention to the road.

There is growing evidence that cell phones distract drivers and cause risks for themselves and others. The cell-savvy user never uses a mobile phone while driving unless it is "hands free." Without a "hands free" device, you should adopt "Drive Now—Talk Later."

Volume: Speak softly.

The cell savvy user is careful to speak in hushed tones, knowing that a mobile phone has a sensitive microphone capable of picking up a soft voice. The savvy user also sets the ring tone at a low level with a tune that is soft, gentle, and not annoying. The more crowded the situation, the quieter and softer the volume of voice and ring.

Proximity: Keep your distance.

Each person is surrounded by a personal space. This space provides feelings of safety and calm, especially in crowded places. The smart cell phone user respects the personal space of other people and tries to speak in places 10 to 20 feet or more away from the closest person.

Content: Keep business private.

Many personal and business conversations contain information that should remain confidential or private. Before using a cell phone in a public location to discuss private business or issues, the cell savvy user makes sure that there will be enough distance to keep the content private. Some stories some issues and some conflicts should be saved for times and locations that will allow for confidentiality.

Tone: Keep a civil and pleasant tone.

The cell savvy user knows that others might overhear a conversation, and they are careful to maintain a public voice that will not disturb others. Also, the savvy user knows that certain types of conversations may require or inspire some tough talk or emotional tones. They reserve these conversations for more private settings.

Location: Pick your spot.

Some locations are better for conversations than others. They offer more privacy and less noise. By keeping the cell phone turned off much of the time, the smart cell phone user is able to handle incoming calls under good conditions rather than struggling against interference of various kinds such as flight announcements in the hallways of an airport.

Timing: No cell phone before its time.

The cell savvy user thinks about when to turn the phone on or off. There are many situations where it would be rude if a phone rang, interrupting the transaction at hand or the person with whom you are speaking with in person.

Multi-Tasking: One thing at a time.

Some folks are better at juggling many tasks at the same time than others, but there are some things in life that deserve your full attention. The busy person multi-tasking at a desk can be a wonderful model of efficiency, handling the phone, keyboard, coffee cup and remote control all at the same time, but at other times, multi-tasking can be hazardous, rude and inefficient. The cell savvy user often stops other activities, such as typing, when a call comes through in order to give the caller his/her full attention. Free of distraction, the savvy user makes the most of the call.

Pagers and Their Uses

A pager is a dedicated RF (radio frequency) device that allows the pager user to receive messages broadcast on a specific frequency over a special network of radio- base stations.

The first pager-like system was used in 1921 by the Detroit Police Department. The pager did not win FCC approval until 1958.

The term "pager" was first used in 1959, referring to a Motorola radio communications product: a small receiver that delivered a radio message individually to those carrying the device. The first consumer pager (as we are familiar with them today) was introduced in 1974. It had no display and could not store messages, but it was portable and notified the wearer that a message had been sent.

By 1980, there were 3.2 million pager users worldwide. By 1990, wide-area paging had been invented and more than 22 million pagers were in use. By 1994, there were more than 61 million pagers in use and pagers had become popular for personal use and peaked in the United States at between 45 and 48 million while the number of cell phones had climbed to more than 55 million.

Pagers were considered the most popular form of wireless communication in the country until 1998 when the increased use of cellular phones signaled their decline. Today, industry analysts estimate the number of pagers being used is about 28 million, a significantly lower figure than the approximately 180 million cell phones that were in use.

"There is still a demand for pagers but the number of units being used could drop to about 10 million within the next five years," says Bob Lougee, vice president of corporate communication for Arch Wireless, Inc. of Westborough, Mass.

Uses of pagers today include:
- Health-care industry including patient registration
- Transportation industry
- Government agencies
- Restaurant industry
- Nursery and childcare in houses of worship
- Emergency response team
- Even though use of pagers has declined in the United States, they are still a viable communications tool.

PDAs and Their Uses

PDAs are personal digital assistants, usually designed to fit in one's pocket, which can store documents, spreadsheets, calendar entries, games, databases, and other resources normally associated with a laptop or desktop computer. The difference is that PDAs are relatively inexpensive, highly portable, and are designed to utilize small, low-bandwidth files and applications.

A typical PDA has no keyboard, relying instead on special hardware and pen-based computer software to enable the recognition of handwritten input, which is entered on the surface of a liquid crystal display screen. In addition to including such applications as a word processor, spreadsheet, calendar, and address book, PDAs are used as notepads, appointment schedulers, and wireless communicators for sending and receiving data, faxes, and electronic-mail messages. Introduced in 1993, PDAs achieved only modest acceptance during the remainder of the decade due to their relatively high price and limited applications.

Two big changes in the past few years:

- In 1998, for many purchasers, a PDA/palmtop computer was a serious low-budget alternative to a laptop.
- In 1998, nearly all PDA/palmtops were personal purchases. They may have been used for work, but they were not exclusively for work and were unlikely to have been paid for by employers. In 2004, there is still a consumer market, however, there is also a large corporate vertical market. Many PDA users are given a PDA by their employer, with a degree of personal use being tolerated (i.e., personal e-mail).

Why use a PDA?
Organization: Combines address book, electronic calendar, notepad, documents, doodle pad, to-do list, diary, secret codes and passwords, alarm clock, timer, and more in one small, searchable device.

Is very easy to use, easy to back up to your PC, and to share data with others via infrared port beaming or the Internet.

Can use thousands of applications that allow you to do lots of other things like read and send e-mail, view web pages, documents, spreadsheets, databases, charts, and many other documents.

Can store a lot of text data, such as entire books, and smaller portions of multimedia such as movies, audio, and graphics.

Games (oops, probably should not have mentioned this one!)

Used by financial professionals to manage billing and expenses.

PDAs flexibility is ideal for busy professionals who rely on others to maintain their calendar, utilize group-scheduling functions, or need to maintain an accurate record of important dates or events.

Applications and Uses of PDA's
Interactive PDA technology presents hundreds of new possibilities in marketing and business communications, including:

- Marketing and sales collateral for business meetings.
- Video-based product demonstrations.
- Individual and group talent demonstrations featuring music videos, live performances, television, and film portfolios.
- Realtor property tours and introductions.
- Company overview and/or corporate presentations.
- Genealogical histories with archival photos and video profiles.

- E-commerce resource for products and services.

- Mobile resource for doctors to describe medical treatments and procedures to patients and colleagues.

PDA Buyers Guide

If you are in the market to purchase a PDA, check the following web site for buyer's tips and hints:

http://www.pdabuyersguide.com/tips/palm_vs_pocketpc.htm

Keep Current

To keep up with what's new and cool in the world of handheld computers, visit product websites (many of which offer free e-newsletters) and the following information/newsletter sites:

Epinions.com	http://www.epinions.com
PalmOne	http://www.palmone.com
Happy Palm	http://www.palmstation.com
Palm Infocenter	http://www.palminfocenter.com
Palm Tipsheet	http://www.palmtipsheet.com
Palm Station	http://www.palmstation.com
PDA Geek Newsletter	http://www.geek.com/pdageek/pdamain.htm
PDA Street	http://www.pdastreet.com
The Gadgeteer	http://www.the-gadgeteer.com
Woody's Palm Watch	http://www.woodyswatch.com/palm

This list is by no means complete. It represents a smattering of the informational sites on PDA's, their products, and their use available on the Web.

The Shape of Things to Come

This author has merely scratched the surface regarding PDAs. With the events of the PDA market over the last three years, it would seem that we have pretty well seen the last of keyboard based palmtop computers. Miniaturized but fully functional desktop computers (aka laptops) have won the carry-it-about-computer market, and one handed document viewers with limited editing capacities have won the put-it-in-your-pocket-computer market. Of course, there will remain a niche demand for something different, for something pocketable on which a book could be written. This, however, will be satisfied by third-party software and accessories, such as folding keyboards, expansion memory and, one day soon I expect, external screens that can be rolled or folded away.

"Imagination is more important than knowledge." Therefore, use imagination to enhance your communication skills and those who are in your charge.

Chapter 12

Strategic Communication:
Promoting Your Faith Community in Good Faith

By Donn James Tilson

Introduction

> **One good deed, dying tongueless,**
> **Slaughters a thousand waiting upon that.**
> —*The Winter's Tale*, **William Shakespeare**

A faith group often has information it wants to communicate to key audiences—its own active members, those on the inactive list, those in the ecumenical and interfaith communities, and those in the community. The group will sometimes want to communicate through local media.

With that information, the faith group may seek to persuade:
- a given audience to change an attitude or behavior;
- its active members to grow in their stewardship;
- its inactive members to worship more regularly and to participate in service projects;
- the ecumenical or interfaith community to engage in common projects.
- The faith group may also seek to provide answers to the searching questions of those who are not part of a faith community.

   To what do these efforts amount?—Evangelization-communication or devotional-promotional communication.

As Tilson and Chao note in *The Journal of Media and Religion*, devotional-promotional communication "that is religious in nature may seek to instill great love or loyalty, enthusiasm, or zeal for a particular religious individual, living or deceased, a faith-based institution, or a specific faith."[1] Most important, such communication proceeds within a covenantal relationship based on the foundation of trust, which is essential to its success. Communication that establishes and maintains quality relations between the faith group and its audiences also can be persuasive or promotional in nature. The desire to be both relational and promotional need not be mutually exclusive, and may, in fact, enhance one another.

Devotional-promotional communication need not, and should not, focus exclusively on costly efforts, like advertising or direct mail. There are many inexpensive and creative communication tools that a faith group can use as it seeks to not only deepen the faith of its members but also to bring its message to those who have not heard.

After this introduction, the material in this chapter focuses on two main tools – public relations and advertising. There are many resources available to help you – both books and Internet Web sites – and you'll find these listed throughout this chapter.

Resources:

A Step-by-Step Guide to Church Marketing: Breaking Ground for the Harvest, by Barna, George. Ventura, Calif.: Regal Books, 1992.

Check your Image: A Public Relations Manual for Church Growth by Holcomb, Tim J. and Hayes, Judi S., compilers. Nashville, Tenn.: Convention Press, 1990.

Driving Brand Value: Using Integrated Marketing to Manage Profitable Stakeholder Relationships, by Duncan, Tom and Moriarty, Sandra. New York, N.Y.: McGraw Hill, 1997.

How to Advertise Your Church. Lubbock, Texas,: Net Results.

How to Write a Successful Marketing Plan: A Disciplined and Comprehensive Approach, by Hiebing, Roman G., Jr. and Cooper Scott W., Lincolnwood, Ill: NTC Business, 1997.

Ideabook, design and marketing ideas for desktop publishing, web design and small business, www.ideabook.com

Introduction to Marketing Communications: An Integrated Approach, by Burnett, John and Moriarty, Sandra. Upper Saddle River, NJ: Prentice Hall, 1998.

Marketing Communications Management, by Murphy, John H. and Cunningham, Isabella. Lincolnwood, IL: NTC Contemporary Books, 1999.

Saintly Campaigning: Devotional-Promotional Communication and the U.S. Tour of St. Thérèse's Relics, by Tilson, Donn James and Chao, Yi-Yuan. *Journal of Media and Religion* (Vol. 1, Number 2, 2002), pp. 81-104.

Social Marketing: Improving the Quality of Life, by Kotler, Philip, Roberto, Ned, and Lee, Nancy. Thousand Oaks, CA: Sage Publications, Inc., 2002 (second edition).

Strategic Brands Communications Campaigns, by Schultz, Don E. and Barnes, Beth E. Lincolnwood, IL: NTC Contemporary Books, 1999.

Marketing for Churches and Ministries, by Stevens, Robert E., and Loudon, David L. New York: The Haworth Press, 1992

Marketing for Congregations: Choosing to Serve People More Effectively, by Shawchuck, Norman, Kotler, Philip, and Wren, Bruce. Nashville, Tenn. Abingdon Press, 1992.

Marketing for Non-profit Organizations, by Kotler, Philip (second edition), Englewood Cliffs, N.J.: Prentice-Hall, Inc., 1982.

Rocking the Ages: The Yankelovich Report on Generational Marketing, by Smith, J. Walker and Clurman, Ann. New York: HarperCollins Publishers, Inc., 1997

Selling the Invisible: A Field Guide to Modern Marketing, by Beckwith, Harry. New York: Warner Books, 1997.

Selling Out the Church: The Dangers of Church Marketing, by Kenneson, Philip D., and Street, James L. Nashville, Tenn.: Abingdon Press, 1997.

Public Relations

As Virginia Randall once noted in an article in *PRWeek*, "Religion and public relations go way back. Moses pioneered the concept of the top 10 list (a staple of press releases and late night TV)."[2] That might be stretching the definition of the profession a bit but, public relations is an age-old concept.

Public relations, as a communication discipline, is the work of telling an organization's story to different "publics" in order to foster goodwill and understanding. "Publics" are the audiences you target to receive messages about your faith community. The core of public relations work is relationship management. As the Public Relations Society of America declared at its 1998 Assembly, "Public relations helps an organization and its publics adapt mutually to each other." There are different types of public relations—including community relations, media relations, special events, crisis communication, and employee communication.

Public relations can be quite intentional, but also unintentional. The way you maintain your parking lot, for example, tells a story. Each member of your faith group can be telling a story—good or bad—about your group. It is important to be aware of the intentional and unintentional communications that are sent.

One of the difficulties in doing public relations is that you often lack control over how the story gets covered, or if it gets covered at all. It is also difficult to measure the impact of public relations work, since it is hard to quantify good will. Nonetheless, there are many advantages to understanding public relations and applying the principles of public relations to the communication efforts of your congregation.

Public Relations Planning

There are four steps involved in systematically shaping and maintaining the reputation of your faith community:

- Research and planning
- Action
- Communication
- Evaluation

Research and Planning

If we liken the public relations process to a trip, the first thing we must do is determine where we are now: the starting point or benchmark. Then we determine where we want to go—the destination or objective. Research helps establish these points. We then plan what we will do and say to get from our starting point to our destination. If you are starting a public relations process from scratch, you and members of your faith group need to begin your research by answering three questions:

- What is your faith group's reason for being?
- What people and areas does your faith group serve?
- What services does your faith group provide?

Answers to these questions should give you the basis for a mission statement, as described in chapter one. Such a statement of purpose lays the foundation for your program of action and communication, the next two steps in the public relations process.

Once your faith group's mission is clear, continue your public relations research by conducting a communications audit (as outlined in chapter one) particularly if you have never done one or if it's been several years since your last audit. This will give you an in-depth look of how you communicate with others and how they communicate with you. Specifically, you should determine:

- What do people in your service area know about your church or faith group now?

- How did they find out what they know?

- What do your members know and think about themselves?

- What do you want people to know about your faith group?

- What do you want to know about your group?

- How do people you want to influence receive information?

To get these answers, you will have to gather information from sources inside your organization and from your communities. Information gathering can be divided into four basic research types: formal, informal, primary, and secondary.

Formal research uses "scientific" techniques, such as probability (random) sampling, to gather results that can be said to represent the views of an entire population within a known margin of error. Public opinion polls, such as those conducted by the Gallup Organization, are examples of this type of research. Formal research generally yields quantitative results in numbers or percentages.

Informal research is gathering information by informal (non-random) polls and talking to neighbors, members of the congregation or key community leaders. Informal research yields qualitative results—trends, feelings, ideas about attitudes. These results cannot be said to represent the views of everyone in a target group.

Primary research is collecting information firsthand—doing your own survey or interviews, looking at old newspaper clippings, consulting public records or organizational reports.

Secondary research is using information collected by others such as the U.S. Census data or polling results.

None of these information-gathering approaches is necessarily better than the others. You can often find out what you need to know by informally talking to people in the group you are trying to influence or by using data about opinions from published polls.

Once you determine what your reputation is and what you want it to be, you can decide what to do and say to influence people. You will want to reinforce the positive opinions that people in target groups have of your faith group. You may want to shape the views of target audiences that have no clear image of your group. You will want to lessen the influence of negative opinions.

Determining exactly who you are trying to reach and influence is essential. Few faith groups have the resources to reach all groups. Consequently, you should divide the total potential audience into smaller groups based on characteristics such as age, gender, interests, and location. Rank these groups in order of their importance to your plan. Keep segmenting until the most important audience to be reached is also the smallest in your hierarchy. You should concentrate the greatest portion of your actions, communications and resources on influencing that tightly defined group.

Public relations is built on actions that bring members of key audiences into contact with members of your faith group or ideas your group supports. Actions—such as programs to attract neighbors into your place of worship or public stands on issues such as drug abuse—establish and shape what people in target audiences think of your faith community.

Action

Suit the action to the word; the word to the action;
with this special observance, that you o'erstep not the modesty of nature.
—*Hamlet*, William Shakespeare

The old saying "Actions speak louder than words" is true. If your actions do not back up your words, you lose credibility and the ability to be effective examples to your faith. Therefore, if you say you have a warm friendly place of worship that welcomes visitors, the behavior of your members must reflect that statement.

Continuing the trip analogy, every person—members as well as leaders—needs to be going in the same direction down the same road. If someone takes a wrong turn, the entire effort may fail.

Communication

Christians often call the communication step of the public relations process "witnessing." Communication lets people in target audiences know what your faith group is doing. The goal is to send the appropriate message through the appropriate channel to the right audience to achieve the planned effect. The message is based on actions and beliefs of your faith group.

The communication portion of the public relations plan should address what messages will be sent, by what means, to what audiences, before, during, and after an action or event. Far too often people planning religious activities concentrate solely on advance publicity. They want to build awareness among potential participants and motivate people to come. But messages sent during and after an event can multiply the number of people who know what happened. In that way these messages extend the effects of an action beyond the participants.

The techniques and media you use to send messages before, during, and after an event depend on your public relations objectives. For example, you might mail cards to a small group of community leaders with news of how much money was collected in a special offering for a local homeless shelter. You might rely on telephone calls to deliver information to key religious leaders about a change in meeting arrangements. You might send a news release to your local newspaper to declare your congregation's stand on a pressing social issue. Furthermore, you might discuss that stand with legislators one-on-one.

Communication can be accomplished at times by not saying anything. Silence may, in fact, influence some key audiences more than stating a public position.

Evaluation

Evaluate your work. Were you within your time frame? Were you within budget? Evaluation must be part of every phase of the public relations process, but at the end of the process, you need an overall assessment:

- How well did you implement the plan?

- What results did your plan generate?

- How did your effort influence your target audiences?

You will need to utilize some research tools in order to accurately answer these questions. At the very least, you should review your ongoing public relations efforts annually, asking such questions as: "What have we done? Where should we be going?" In looking back in order to look ahead (just like making your New Year's resolutions), always refer to your mission statement and the results of your latest communications audit as well as the public relations plan for each particular project or program.

Public Relations Plan

Public relations plans are based on quality research and are the roadmap for your project or program. Such plans tell why you are doing what you are doing, who you are trying to influence, what you are trying to communicate, and by what media you will communicate.

The plan provides:
- Step-by-step strategies, tactics, and key messages.

- Timetables of when and how steps will be taken.

- Who is going to do the work.

- Cost of the plan.

- The expected results.

- Methods by which the plan will be evaluated.

Public relations plans are built on objectives that support an overall goal and can be pro-active or reactive depending on the situation that your faith group faces. Plan objectives tell you what you intend to accomplish within a specific time and can be short-range, medium-range, or long-range in nature.

Public relations objectives involve:

Awareness: exposing target audiences to your messages. However, you do not know if people in those groups noticed, received, or understood those messages.

Example: To deliver information about our vacation Bible school to 5,000 households during June through at least one news story in the local newspaper.

Recognition: exposing target audiences to your messages and making sure people in those groups notice them.

Example: To increase our congregation's name recognition among North Side residents by 10 percent during the next three months.

Comprehension: exposing target audiences to your messages and making sure people in those groups notice and understand them.

Example: To enhance understanding of our faith group's stand on ministry to the disabled community among our members by 50 percent over the next 12 months.

Opinions: what people say they think about a topic.

Example: To increase support in our congregation for construction of a new education building by 50 percent by September 1.

Attitudes: what people like or dislike about a subject.

Example: To increase negative attitudes in our congregation about a state lottery by 50 percent before the election.

Behavior: an observable action.

Example: To attract at least 100 first-time visitors to our worship services over the next 12 months.

Objectives must be specific and measurable. Establish specific objectives such as: "We will bring in 60 new members into our fellowship within the next 12 months." Objectives also should be attainable. For example, don't set an objective "To increase weekly attendance at fellowship by 50 percent within the next six months" unless you realistically can achieve that. In addition, the number of objectives should be realistic. Three to six may be more than enough for one year.

Public Relations Plan Outline

Here is an outline of a public relations plan. Such a plan would be the result of your work in the planning process described in the previous section. Follow the design of this plan and provide adequate information and details to make it workable and helpful for your faith group.

1. Situation

Clear statement of the problem you are addressing.

Analysis of the situation – factors causing the problem, groups affected by the problem, strengths and weaknesses of the organization, threats, opportunities (your SWOT analysis, as discussed in chapter one).

Identification of target audiences you want to influence through your actions to address this problem.

2. Goal

What is the overall goal, issue or problem that your plan addresses?

3. Objectives

What specific steps will help attain the goal?

4. Implementation

How are you going to accomplish your objectives?

Who is going to do each task?

What is the time table for these actions?

Who is responsible for monitoring and coordinating the effort?

What could go wrong, and how will you respond if it does?

5. Communication

Who are the target audiences?

What messages do we want each target audience to receive?

6. Budget

What will each effort cost?

7. Evaluation

How will you assess what you did?

In evaluating your plan, you should look not only at the outputs of your efforts (what you did to expose your audiences to your message) but also at the outcomes of your work (what really happened as a result of your plan). Refer to the "Evaluative Methods" outline in this chapter for a list of ways to measure your activities.

Such a plan is often referred to as Management by Objective plan (or MBO plan). You can outline your plan, charting each component in an easy-to-read format, and give each member of your team a copy. That will ensure that everyone "is singing off the same page" and provide your team leader with a checklist to monitor that things stay on track. We have included an example of an MBO chart for you to follow as a guide. On that chart, you may want to include "Cost" as an additional column so you can identify the cost of each component of your plan and determine your total budget. For more information on planning, refer to the strategic communications plan discussed in chapter one.

To find out more about public relations, contact the Public Relations Society of America, 33 Maiden Lane, New York, N.Y. 10038, (212/995-2230) (www.prsa.org).

Management by Objective

Goal:	To gain attention and support of Dade County Public High Schools for Butler Basketball School and recruit tutors for after-school tutoring program via Campus Media Team							
Themeline: "Elevate your game through education"								
Reporting Unit Objectives	**Specific Audience**	**Message**	**Action/Communication**	**Priority**	**Initiate**	**Complete**	**Responsibility**	
Establish Contact with Athletic Directors and Principals and get at least 10 schools to respond	Athletic Directors & Principals in the Miami-Dade Public School System	BBS is a good beneficial program and needs support from schools to activate it	Type, copy, put together and mail packets that include information about BBS and make follow-up calls and letters	1	Oct. 23, 2003	Ongoing	Angie	
Recruit at least 15 volunteers/tutors for BBS by tabling on campus at University Center	University of Miami graduates and undergraduates	Tutoring position available in Math & English and other areas; paid position	*Tabling in UC: use cookies and candy *Flyers advertising need for tutors in Schools and around campus *Updating tutor database sheet on BBS site	2	Oct. 27, 2003	Oct. 29, 2003	Marianne, Anisha	
Distribute flyers to: 8 Schools/Buildings 3 Campus Dorms 1 Sorority Society 1 Student Volunteer Service	University of Miami graduates and undergraduates	Tutoring position available in Math & English and other areas; paid position or can be volunteer	Distribute flyers advertising need for tutors at BBS; place them on bulletin boards, hand them to office secretaries	3	Nov. 10, 2003	Nov. 21, 2003	Nicole, Jenn	

Media Relations

In order to increase coverage about your faith community, you may want to develop personal relationships with media staff that cover religion and religious activities. Such relationships may result in your becoming an expert the reporter turns to for particular faith-based issues. You may also want to help leaders in your faith group know how to be interviewed and how to handle questions from the media.

Begin by listing the people who handle news sent from your congregation. Send each of them a brief letter suggesting a week or day you would like to meet with them. Follow up with a phone call for a specific appointment when no deadlines or assignments are pressing.

Remember media people are (as we all are) different. Some are more inclined to publish news about mosque, synagogue, temple, or church activities. Others are more interested in religious issues that span many faith groups. Large newspapers will have specific persons assigned as religion editors. Smaller papers will give a single reporter many assignments, including religion.

You should also get to know the city editor—the person who decides how much space a given story is worth, if any, and someone you can contact if the religion writer is out. On smaller papers, the city editor may be the person you deal with regularly. Also, get to know assignment editors at local television stations.

Study your situation and act accordingly, but remember different media have different needs. Newspapers, for example, use news stories, but also letters to the editor, editorials, Sunday supplements, and special-interest sections.

Broadcast media have news programs, talk shows, call-in programs, community bulletin boards, and other programs.

Any person is motivated by self-interest. News people have space and broadcast time to fill; they need an unending flow of material. Learn how to help them see the value in what you have to offer in relation to other things competing for their attention.

Many secular media persons recoil from contact by religious organization, not because they are anti-religious, but because they have been badgered and manipulated by religious representatives who did not try to learn their preferences, treat them respectfully, deal honestly with them, produce competently prepared news releases, fact sheets or press kits, or practice the key to good media relations—helpfulness. It is also helpful (when appropriate) to function as a reliable resource person for them.

News is what journalists on a given publication or station consider as timely, interesting, and important. Around news offices, the saying is, "News is what the editor says it is." News media do not exist to do publicity for you—no matter how important it is to you to make your information available to the public. News media exist to report news. If the news publicizes some event or development as a side effect, that is okay. But if you ask a reporter to publicize a specific event, you may lose credibility.

Figure out the news content of your project, event or cause, and approach news media on that basis. Then supplement your news efforts with publicity through such channels as bulletin boards, newsletters, mail, signs, public service announcements, telephone calls, and bumper stickers.

It is up to you to discover the varying meanings of news in your locale. News for one type of medium may not be news to others. A weekly newspaper may banner something on page one that a metropolitan daily would omit. Television and radio have different standards. Significance and interest varies between size, type, scope, format, audience, and location of the medium.

What about debatable issues? A religion writer on a major paper declares that one of the biggest problems in getting religious news published involves religion communicators' concern over their own image. They get so protective they damage their credibility. Long-time religious media professional Robert L. Friedly advises: "Include contrary opinions and points of debate in your coverage of congregational events, as well as welcoming first-hand coverage by media personnel. This produces credibility with your constituency as well as the press. The agony-ecstasy struggle with tough moral, theological and social questions should be, as much as possible, open to all. Such openness makes for a healthier community and puts the congregation in a proper servant role."

That leads us to a game plan for controversy. Religion communicators, while under no obligation to air all their dirty laundry, do have the obligation to practice honesty and integrity. Sometimes they must walk a tightrope in deciding where the greater good lies. Controversial news often has a negative effect, but it can affect a religious institution positively. This can be seen when people see the institution's willingness to take a stand, assume responsibilities in the world, act for its spiritual cause and the benefit of others, and even suffer criticism for righteousness' sake (see Chapter 13 on "crisis communications").

You may be as open and prolific with your news as you wish, but if you feel the need to face every issue with too much information or a ready news release, your media relations will become laughable and perish from overexposure. More than one editor has admitted that mail from certain organizations end up in the trash because the sources have long since outworn their welcome with a series of trivial news releases. That includes overuse of news conferences. They sound like a glamorous way to do business, but too many of them not only waste time but can make you sound like the "boy who cried wolf" if you call conferences indiscriminately. Use news conferences rarely, and, then only in cases of widespread media interest or extremely limited time on an important subject or crisis situation. News releases and/or interviews by reporters usually work better.

Once you have placed information with a member of the media, do not call immediately unless you have a legitimate reason to add information or clarify an item. If in doubt, do not call. Follow-up phone calls to see if busy reporters have received material or will run your story will soon wear out your welcome. A word to the wise: wait and watch; be available to provide follow-up assistance and stay out of the way until that time comes.

Do not demand a correction unless absolutely necessary. Research has shown that only 5 to 10 percent of readers see a story, according to Communications Briefings (Encoders Inc.) If it appears again with a rebuttal or correction, 20 to 25 percent will see it. Repetitions of negative issues can cause the public to gravitate toward the negative. Find other ways to set the record straight.

Avoid embarrassing reporters or chipping away at their credibility, but do not be afraid to tell them in a diplomatic way about serious errors—not minor ones. Send letters of thanks for a good job, with copies to supervisors. If you must point out errors, it is best to talk to the reporter, rather than putting it in print. Good media and human relations must go on after a given incident has faded away.

Seizing the moment is a principle to use any time the moment is right to generate news before an opportunity evaporates, but it has a special significance to religion communicators. The secular news media's purpose is not to communicate your messages or beliefs, so do not thrust it upon them. But, occasionally, There are moments when the content of your message intersects with news.

News releases are a mainstay in media relations. To learn how to write and format a news release, turn to chapter three. You may also visit the University of Otago's (New Zealand) Web site (www.online.wbc.org/docs/market/mk_campaign_pr.html) for more tips on news releases and information on media relations in general.

Signs

Signage in and around your buildings isn't the first thing that comes to mind when you think about public relations. Yet a good sign is a silent evangelist pointing toward a sacred space where people come to relate to their faith and each other. It can be indifferent or it can be friendly. The signs inside your building can be confusing or cheerful. Don't underestimate the importance of proper signage for impressing visitors, assimilating new members and encouraging the long-timers.

Begin by taking an inventory of the signs both on your property and inside your building. Is your logo being used on the main exterior identification sign? Is it on you interior directional signs? Is it important to include a denominational reference?

What materials are they made of? What is their condition? Note the color of the background and the color of the lettering. Note the type styles. Are the words in capital letters or upper and lower case letters? Note how various signs are mounted. How could your signs be improved? Would they be more effective if they were moved higher or lower or to a new location?

Some signs become outdated because of new construction or changes in traffic patterns and should be removed altogether. As room use changes inside the building, some temporary signs become more permanent than they should. Try to keep the perspective of a first-time visitor. Would that visitor become confused or misdirected by a particular sign? Does the condition of the sign give a bad image?

Be intentional about how you display your signs. Do they match the décor and architecture of the building? Do you want signs to express simplicity or richness? Are color and type styles coordinated?

Do your outdoor signs have a logical location for the greatest visibility to people in cars and pedestrians? Do they provide immediate information?

The main exterior sign creates the first impression of your faith group. An ugly sign in need of repair is worse than no sign at all. Construction materials can range from a inexpensive painted plywood sign to an expensive interior lighted sign. Drive up and down the street at average speed and look at your sign. It should be easily picked out of the highway clutter with lettering that can be read as you drive by. In the commercial world a new sign is worth a 20 percent increase in business.

Signs that contain information such as the times of worship, activities, sermon topics and telephone numbers should be on a separate sign and in a location where the reader can pull out of traffic and write down the information.

Exterior signs for disabled and visitor parking should be visible, but they should not compete with the main sign. These signs, along with entrance and exit signs should be of similar style and design

Does your main exterior identification sign need to be replaced or repainted? Should a message board or graphic be added? Have traffic patterns changed since the sign was installed? Do trees or shrubbery hide the sign? Are there adequate directional signs for disabled people or visitors? To answer these questions you might want to ask visitors if they had any problem finding their way.

Outbuildings signs may be mounted or painted directly on the building. Formed plastic or cast metal letters can be ordered through a sign shop or catalog. Decide how large these signs need to be by how far they are located from the main building or street.

The second phase involves the main interior directional signs, room identification signs and a floor plan. Study the need for interior signs such as the office, restrooms, nursery and worship space. Are these signs readable from a distance? Would they be more visible hanging from the ceiling or extending from a wall?

Plastic engraved with exposed sub-surface lettering is the most common material for interior signs; they may be purchased at an office supply store, a hardware store, or a sign company. Plastic with applied vinyl lettering can be obtained through mail order companies or at new computer-generated "quickie sign" shops. You can also get adhesive-backed vinyl lettering that can be applied to any smooth surface. For hand-lettered signs on wood, plastic or masonite, go to a professional sign artist or calligrapher.

Lightweight signs can be mounted flush to a smooth surface with double-sided foam tape. Heavier signs and/or rough mounting surfaces may call for glue, liquid nails or mounting brackets.

If your facility is large you many want to install a floor plan with a "You are here" designation. You may then want to color code signs in different areas of the building to coincide with the main directional map.

Also, make sure the existing light is sufficient. If it is not, you may need to find ways to illuminate these signs.

You are now ready to deal with off-premise signs and church vehicle graphics:

Lead people to your faith community through off-premise signs. These signs range from an 18 by 24 inch metal sign to 4 by 8 feet painted signs. These signs rarely cause people to join your faith group, but they help in creating a presence in your community. They also direct people to you for district meetings or rallies.

If you already have directional signs, don't forget to monitor their condition; they may be damaged or leaning. Weeds may also hide the sign or give it an unkempt appearance. Check with the highway department and the local sign ordinances to see if the signs are properly licensed, permitted and insured. Always get permission from the property owner.

You may also lease billboards from outdoor advertising companies by the month or year. You may also arrange to have your sign rotated to various locations. The cost is calculated on the number of people per day who can see your sign and the size. They are most effective for special events and services. Keep it simple, with a creative punch line. Limit the main copy to no more than six or seven words plus your logo. Keep the address and telephone number small. People can pull over and write these down.

Check graphics on vehicles. Vans tend to be neglected, but these vehicles may provide more visibility for your faith community than your building. A new paint job with bright legible lettering can make even an old van look new. Whether your van lettering is vinyl or paint, magnetic or permanent, it should be large, legible, and of high contrast. Avoid Old English and most script-type faces. Maintain a clean and bright appearance. Your van should be a traveling billboard.

The commercial world uses interior and exterior banners effectively. Faith groups can too. The freshness and motion in the wind create interest and excitement. Make the banners bright and colorful and keep the message simple. Some city ordinances restrict certain types of exterior banners. Always consider banners as temporary. They lose their effectiveness and can become shabby if kept too long. The vinyl-lettered sign has become the most popular and least expensive. The painted banner usually has more character. Both banners have about the same endurance. Canvas is heavier, wind resistant and looks better than the plastic wove, but it's more expensive. Plastic wove comes in bright colors, is lightweight, inexpensive and works indoors and out.

Murals are a wonderful way to enhance an ugly exterior wall or make a statement to the neighborhood. Check local ordinances. Hire a local artist who has had experience in murals or a sign company. The artist can also design it and supervise a youth group to paint the mural. Be sure the wall is well-sealed and free from potential water damage.

Special Events

Maybe you're celebrating your faith community's 50th anniversary. Or perhaps it's a bazaar or open house. Whatever the event, it will reflect on your image and membership. According to *Power-Packed PR: Ideas That Work*, "Events do more to change opinions than any other channel."[3] You can't afford to do it wrong. Your special event can have positive results for your faith group.

Special events can provide an opportunity for you to educate people about your faith group and your ministry and can often attract a large crowd, providing you with the opportunity to reach many people at once with your message. For example, each year on January 6, the Feast of the Epiphany (the day on which, according to tradition, John the Baptist baptized Jesus in the Jordan River and during which his divinity was revealed), St. Nicholas Greek Orthodox Church in Tarpon Spring, Fla., celebrates with a special service followed by a procession of area Greek choirs, dance groups, clergy, and city officials to the city's Spring Bayou. After a blessing-of-the-waters liturgy, Greek-American boys dive in the bayou to retrieve a holy cross thrown in the waters by the Archbishop. Festivities continue afterward with Greek dancers and food served in the city's park. The Feast of the Epiphany celebrations regularly attract some 30,000 visitors and generate major local television and newspaper coverage that extends around the nation and the world. According to the *Public Relations Quarterly*, "local government provides an array of support for the event . . . with representatives serving on the organizing committee, working with the chamber, attending in an official capacity, and providing city property as well as police, fire, rescue, and other services."[4]

Promoting your faith group through a special event begins with planning. You will want to set the date, time, site and speakers at least nine months in advance. Many cities now have year-round activities calendars to help plan without conflicting with another organization's event (check with your local library or Chamber of Commerce). You will likely have to plan the event with committee members who have been long-time members of your faith group and are familiar with past events you have held. New members can bring fresh approaches to planning. Be sure to include both. Never plan alone.

Review your prospective audience (both internal and external). Who would most likely support your event? Look at age, income, gender, political leanings and geographic location. This research will help give you an understanding of these publics and the impact they may have on your event's success. It is to your faith group's benefit to take time to do the research right.

Once you know with whom you want to communicate, you must decide on a message. What do you want your audience to know, to feel, or to do? Put your plan on paper describing what is to be done and how to get it done. Who will do publicity? Mailings? Coordination? Dole out assignments taking the gifts and graces of committee members into account (see the planning checklist at the end of this section). Make sure the committee meets at regular intervals to review progress and be sure you are all working toward the agreed-upon goal.

Prepare for possible crises by asking committee member to predict worst-case scenarios that could develop. Then think of strategies to overcome them, should they arise.

One way to make sure your event is successful is to make it attractive to the media. Indicate in your publicity if this is the "largest," "first," or a significant anniversary, or tie your event into a current trend or special day. Choose a memorable name that can be identified positively with your faith group.

After the speeches have been made, the confetti swept up, and the food devoured, evaluate your efforts. Summarize how the event was put together, who did what, how much did it cost, how many attended, weather, and reactions of participants. Keep clips of news articles, copies of aired radio and television news stories as well as your own photos of the event. Keep all this information in a labeled file as a record for church historians and the next planning committee.

Planning checklist for special events

 Use this checklist to assign tasks to committee members and to review tasks that need to be done as you prepare for your special event.

Site
Parking
Health and safety
Transportation
Security
Housekeeping
Conference accommodations
Audio-visuals
Lecterns
Water
Microphones
Guides
Exhibits
Press room and electronic media accommodations
Signs
Telephones
Disabled access
Smoking and non-smoking guest accommodations
Decorations

Publicity
Promotion planning: advertising, public relations, media relations
Television, radio and print news releases
Press kits
Photography
Media credentials
Internal communication
Letters
Printing
Posters and brochures
Programs
Communication center

Hospitality
Food services
VIP suites and accommodations
Guests
Spouse tours
Entertainment
Greeting
Housing
Contests
Prizes
Promotions
Mementos

Finance
Budget
Bookkeeping
Income
Expenses
Insurance
Licensing
Permits

Speakers
Invitations
Photographs
Biographies
Honoraria
Advance information/liaison
Material to be reproduced
Transportation
Thank you correspondence

Reservations
Invitations
Agendas
Program copy
Participants' materials
Name badges
Registration/welcoming
Seating
Tours
Telephone marketing
Message center

Advertising

For years, local faith groups depended almost totally on print advertising as their primary advertising option. It was easy, convenient, and everybody read the newspaper. The most popular print advertisements for faith groups ran on the newspaper's weekly religion page. Today, however, the purchase of print advertising must be well planned and executed to ensure its effectiveness. Print is only one of the advertising media available.

Because the average person assimilates 1,500 messages daily, you must develop and advertising plan that will compete in the marketplace. Before selecting specific options, a faith group should review all options and select only those that fit the overall communication plan.

Some individuals still have negative images of advertising. But advertising affects all of us on a daily basis—in our workplace, home, school and neighborhood. Thus, it is a proven communication tool that faith groups can use positively.

Innovation and quality are the keys to audience response. Effectively done advertisements help create a positive image for your faith group in its community. Hopefully, the image you create with your visual advertising will cause people to react to what they have seen. That is the goal of any advertisement: to produce a positive reaction to your message.

Another important factor to remember is that advertising costs. While some free advertising options are available, a faith group should not depend on those options for its total advertising plan. The plan should be built on paid advertising options, supplemented with non-paid advertising.

Advertising, to be truly effective, must be repetitious. Have you noticed the same advertisements over and over? Major corporations know the value of repetitious advertising. Faith groups must follow the same approach.

Learn as much as you can about your target audience. Demographic information identifies persons by location, ethnic origin, age, gender, economic status, profession, and other important factors. Psychographic information identifies what individuals or specific groups of people believe about issues or how they might respond to a particular issue.

Whenever and wherever a faith group chooses to advertise, the advertisements should be part of a well-planned, well-executed marketing strategy designed to produce long-term results. It also involves long-term commitment by the faith group because sporadic advertising is not cost effective and will lead to frustration by members.

Resources

Becoming a Public Relations Writer, by Smith, Ronald D. Mahwah, N.Y.: Lawrence Erlbaum Associates, Inc., 2003.

Campaign Strategies and Message Design: A Practitioner's Guide From Start to Finish, by Moffitt, Mary Anne. Westport, CT: Praeger Publishers, 1999.

Crisis Communications: A Casebook Approach, by Fearn-Banks, K. Mahwah, N.Y.: Lawrence Erlbaum Associates, Inc., 2002 (second edition).

The Crisis Manager: Facing Risk and Responsibility, by Otto Lerbinger. Mahwah, N.Y.: Lawrence Erlbaum Associates, Inc., 1997.

Handbook of Public Relations, by Heath, R.L. (editor). Thousand Oaks, Calif.: Sage Publications, Inc., 2000.

Not If, But When! (second edition, 1999). The 77-page crisis communication manual prepared by United Methodist Communications may be ordered by calling 800/ 476-7766.

The Practice of Public Relations, by Seitel, Fraser P. Upper Saddle River, N.J.: Prentice Hall, 1998 (seventh edition).

Proposal for a Catholic Radio Station, by Tobin, Richard W., and Tilson, Donn J.. Miami: Archdiocese of Miami Communications Commission, 1989

Public Relations As Relationship Management, by Ledingham, J.A. and Bruning, S. (editors). Mahwah, N.Y.: Lawrence Erlbaum Associates, Inc., 2000.

Public Relations: A Values-Driven Approach, by Guth, David W. and Marsh, Charles. New York, N.Y.: Longman, 2003.

Public Relations Campaign Strategies: Planning for Implementation, by Kendall, Robert. New York, N.Y.: Longman, 1996.

Public Relations Campaigns and Techniques: Building Bridges into the 21st Century, by Matera, Fran and Artigue, Ray J. New York, N.Y.: Longman, 2000.

Public Relations Cases, by Hendrix, J. Belmont, Calif.: Wadsworth/Thomson Learning, 2001 (fifth edition).

Public Relations on the Internet: Winning Strategies to Inform and Influence the Media, the Investment Community, the Government, the Public, and More! by Holtz, Shel. New York: AMACOM, 1999.

Public Relations Strategies and Tactics, by Wilcox, D.L., Ault, P.H., Agee, W., and Cameron, G.T. New York, N.Y.: Longman, 2003 (seventh edition).

Public Relations Worktext: A Writing and Planning Resource, by Zappala, Joseph M. and Carden, Ann R.. Mahwah, N.Y.: Lawrence Erlbaum Associates, Inc., 2004.

Public Relations Writing: Form and Style, by Newsom, Doug and Carrell, Bob. Belmont, Calif.: Wadsworth, 1998 (fifth edition).

Public Relations Writing: The Essentials of Style and Format, by Bivins, Thomas H. Lincolnwood, Ill.: NTC Contemporary Books, 1999 (fourth edition).

Religious Tourism, Public Relations and Church-State Partnerships by Tilson, Donn James. *Public Relations Quarterly* (Fall 2001), pp 35-39

Spinning the Web: A Handbook for Public Relations on the Internet, by Witmer, Diane F.. New York, N.Y.: Longman, 2000.

Strategic Planning for Public Relations, by Smith, Ronald D. Mahwah, N.Y..: Lawrence Erlbaum Associates, Inc., 2002.

Strategic Public Relations Management, by Austin, E.W. and Pinkleton, B.E. Mahwah, N.Y.: Lawrence Erlbaum Associates, Inc., 2001.

Tell It! TM Media Manual: A comprehensive guide to bringing your stories to television, radio and print, a joint project of FACTA NEWS, Inc. and The Lutheran Church-Missouri Synod. St. Louis, Mo.: *FACTA NEWS*, Inc., 1997.

This Is PR: The Realities of Public Relations, by Newsom, D., Turk, J., and Kruckeberg, D. Belmont, Calif.: Wadsworth/Thomson Learning, 2000 (seventh edition).

You'd Better Have a Hose If You Want to Put Out the Fire, by Henry, Rene A. Ames, Iowa: Iowa State University Press, 2000.

When Your Client is God, by Randall, Virginia. *PRWeek* (March 13, 2000), pp. 20-21.

Writing Right for Broadcast and Internet News, by Attkisson, Sharyl and Vaughan, Don R. New York, N.Y.: Longman, 2003.

Print

Writing in *The Media of Mass Communication: 2003 Update*, John Vivian reports that one out of three people in the U.S. reads a newspaper daily, and newspapers are the medium of choice for more advertising than competing media.[5] Additionally, metro daily zoned or neighborhood editions, weekly community newspapers and alternative/minority newspapers (counterculture, foreign-language, ethnic publications) have thrived with suburban sprawl and with those seeking to maintain their own particular identity. Nevertheless, daily newspaper readership is declining as more people turn to television and radio as their primary information sources and as newspapers fail to replace their aging readership. According to Vivian, daily circulation fell 10 million from 1988 to 2000 even as the percentage of Americans below age 35 reading a daily paper fell from 67 percent in 1965 to 30 percent in 1990. Today, newspaper readers tend to be over 40 years of age.

Many newspapers, particularly weeklies or in smaller communities, offer regular listings of faith groups in the community. These should be avoided unless they are very inexpensive or free. The standard weekly advertisement or religion page listing will not have any image building or evangelistic impact. Most persons who see these notices already are faith group members; however, this type of advertisement or listing might appeal to newcomers in the community looking for a worship center of their faith group.

Local advertising agencies can be helpful to a faith group in the production and purchase of advertising. Often, the agency will reduce or forego its fees in return for the commission it receives from the advertising purchased by the faith group.

If, however, the faith group chooses to do its own purchasing, it would be wise for a representative from the group to develop a relationship with an advertising representative at the local newspaper. This relationship can have long-term benefits, especially as the amount of advertising purchased increases. An advertising representative can help the group avoid costly mistakes and work with the placement of the ad. The advertising representative can help secure preferred space and determine if the message will reach its intended audience.

Secure rate cards which list circulation, audience demographics, market ratings and costs. Learn to read the rate card and to compare readership with costs. Do not be afraid to ask questions or to negotiate. If unsure about information or instructions printed in rate cards, ask questions.

Publications with large audiences generally are more effective for advertising than those with smaller audiences. One exception may be those metropolitan areas that have suburban or neighborhood newspapers. Because these are targeted to a specific geographic region and audience, they often can be an effective way to reach people living in the target area. Advertising in these smaller publications is always less expensive

Surprisingly, some faith groups have had limited success with classified advertising. Classified ads are sold by the word or in standard block rates of so many words for a set price. These ads can be effective for drawing attention to an event, a prayer telephone line or other item. Readers don't expect to see an advertisement for "religion" in the classified section of the newspaper.

Most newspapers also have daily or weekly calendars of community events. Listings usually are free to faith groups and are an excellent way to promote special events. They should not be used for regular programs or activities of your group. While these announcements are not effective as image builders for the faith group, they can help with long-term name recognition.

Faith groups also should consider news and advertising placement on newspaper Web sites. Most dailies and many weeklies now have such sites, which, in some cases, are specially-edited versions of their newsprint issue. Newspapers may offer special rates for their Web site editions or "package deals" for advertising in both their print and on-line editions. Still, according to Vivian,[6] many advertisers are hesitant to buy cyber-ads because there isn't a standard measurement of audience and no standard pricing. Hits (visitors who click an on-screen icon) and visits (counts of people who surf into a site) are not necessarily true measures of audience size as people often access a particular site multiple times. However, as the Web becomes accessible to a larger number of U.S. households—more than 40 percent had access in 2000—electronic newspapers will become an important medium for reaching an organization's "cyber-community" with news and ads about its activities.

Although print advertising usually focuses on newspapers, there are other options available, including programs for community events (symphonies, theater, high school athletics) which reach a particular audience. There is no standard rate for these publications, but they often can reach a large audience for a nominal fee.

Broadcast

Many faith groups include radio and television as important media in their overall communication plan. According to John Vivian in *The Media of Mass Communications 2003 Update*, there are more than 11,000 radio stations in the U.S., broadcasting from the largest metropolitan areas to the smallest communities; of these, 10 percent are noncommercial stations operated by colleges and other non-profit institutions.[7] On the AM dial, news-talk radio shows have become the most common format even as FM stations have concentrated on playing a range of music from country western to classical to easy listening. Television is equally a powerful medium with more than 13,280 stations—from commercial and noncommercial to cable systems—blanketing the nation 98 percent of U.S. households have at least one televisions set). The latest television frontier, the Web, now features streaming or broadcasting of video programming to individual computer screens over the Internet.

When it comes to advertising, both media present certain challenges. Radio audiences and radio programs are selective, and advertisements must be placed on the station with the right format. The type of programming used by a radio station is the key factor in determining the station's dominant listener base. Because radio listeners are often doing other things while listening to the radio, advertisements must attract and hold the listener's attention. The cost of producing and airing television ads can be prohibitive for many. Do not let costs, however, scare you off from considering adding television ads to your marketing mix.

Local groups might make use of radio or television commercials produced by and made available through the national offices of their faith group. Often a local tag line is added to these spots (e.g., "brought to you by the Church of the Brethren in Independence"). Since producing radio and television commercials can be very costly, local faith groups should begin by consulting the national communication office of their faith group to determine if any are already available. These ready-to-go materials might be available for nominal or no cost.

Obviously, local groups can work with advertising agencies or local stations to prepare their own radio or television commercials. Station advertising representatives can assist with researching demographics, picking time slots and producing the ad.

In addition to commercials, local groups may make use of ready-to-use broadcasts made available regionally or nationally. One example is Lutheran Vespers, a weekly program that is broadcast on 230 stations in the U.S. and also overseas. The radio ministry of the Evangelical Lutheran Church in America has been on the air continuously since 1947. A Lutheran congregation might buy air time on a local radio station and place this half-hour program or the station might offer free air time for the broadcast. Either way, the local congregation is likely to include a tag line at the end of the broadcast, identifying the local sponsor and perhaps including an invitation to worship with the congregation.

Local faith communities also can broker (rent) air time on area stations to broadcast their own programming. As financial support and audience for the broadcasts increase, the length of the on-air programming can be expanded. For example, the Archdiocese of Miami, following a plan developed by its Communications Commission to create a radio ministry[8] brokered a two-hour program in Spanish on a local AM stations in 1990. The program soon expanded to four hours, moved to a six-hour slot on another AM station two years later, and, by 1993, was part of a 13-hour daily broadcast in English, Spanish, Creole, and Portuguese on yet another AM station. Later the English-language programming was split off and aired with brokered time on a second AM station.

Of course, there's always the possibility of starting your own radio station. Certain community groups around the country—African-Americans in Louisiana, fishermen in Chesapeake Bay, and migrant workers in Florida—have done just that with the help of a national organization called the Prometheus Radio Project, based in Philadelphia. According to Richard Brand in the Miami Herald, in December 2003, Prometheus organized a radio "barn raising" for the Coalition of Immokalee Workers who obtained a federal license to run a community radio station.[9] Dozens of Prometheus volunteers came to the small farming town and in a single weekend built a 100-watt low-power station (3-to-5-mile broadcast radius) at the coalition's downtown headquarters. Seminars followed for the migrant workers on digital editing, station governance and fundraising. Now, the station airs news and information programming in Spanish and indigenous languages such as Zapotec and Quiche, giving local people a voice in their community (Brand, 2003).

In addition to commercials and broadcast sponsorships, some faith groups seek local placement of public service announcements (PSAs). PSAs are intended to provide a message of interest and benefit to the larger secular community. Any image enhancement for the sponsoring group that comes from a PSA is a secondary benefit. Radio and television stations often determine whether or not to use an organization's PSA based on the following criteria:

- Does the sponsor have a good reputation (questions of honesty, integrity)?
- Is the PSA message about an important social problem or public event?
- Is the PSA creative, original, and exciting?

Television stations, additionally, look at PSAs produced by national organizations to see if there's a local angle—those that offer a local telephone number or a way to receive information on the local chapter have a better chance of being aired than those that don't include such information. Local television stations also prefer to air PSAs from organizations involved in community activities similar to those that the station regularly sponsors. PSAs usually require a long lead time. Television stations should be contacted two to three months in advance of the scheduled event while radio stations may require three weeks or more advance notice.

Many congregations use PSAs to get an unbelievable amount of free radio and television air time. Stations are not required to use everything sent to them; sometimes the "bake sale" kind of notice ends up in the trash. Stations do try hard to serve religious and non-profit groups. It is up to you to keep abreast of the various radio and television stations; requirements and formats will vary. Type everything accurately and neatly, spell correctly and be sure of names, times and addresses. Double-space and be sure to include your name as a contact with daytime and evening phone numbers. Keep PSAs short and accurate. Before your consider PSAs for television, contact your local television station to get its guidelines for PSAs. Professionally produced PSAs tend to be best, but even a simple color slide accompanied by appropriate voice-over is acceptable in smaller markets. The following PSA for radio may be used as a guide in preparing yours.

Public Service Announcement: Time: 45-seconds

From: Miami Children's Hospital   Contact: Donn J. Tilson
3000 S.W. 62 Avenue   Community Relations Director
Miami, Florida 33155   (305) 666-2000

For Immediate Release

ANNCR: MIAMI CHILDREN'S HOSPITAL, ERICSSON CHAMPIONSHIP TENNIS PLAYERS AND HOT-105 WILL SERVE IT UP FOR CHARITY AT A BENEFIT DINNER ON KEY BISCAYNE THIS SATURDAY NIGHT. TENNIS CELEBRITIES WILL SERVE AN ITALIAN DINNER FROM FIVE TO SEVEN THIRTY HOSTED BY THE OLIVE GARDEN AT THE ERIC-SSON PLAYERS CHAMPIONSHIPS. TICKETS ARE 50 DOLLARS AND INCLUDE DINNER AND RESERVED SEATS FOR SATURDAY NIGHT'S MATCHES. ALL PROCEEDS BENEFIT MIAMI CHILDREN'S HOSPITAL. FOR RESERVATIONS, CALL SIX-SIX-SIX-TWO-EIGHT-EIGHT-NINE (666-2889). SEATING IS LIMITED SO CALL NOW. THAT'S SIX-SIX-SIX-TWO-EIGHT-EIGHT-NINE (666-2889). ONCE AGAIN, GET SERVED BY ERICSSON'S TENNIS STARS THIS SATURDAY NIGHT TO BENEFIT MIAMI CHILDREN'S HOSPITAL.

Some faith groups broadcast weekly worship services or put together their own show of religious music and programming. There are measurable results. A group can do a great deal to impress a community with its friendly spirit, its broadening concerns, and its responsiveness. It helps if the sermons are good. You must have a volunteer or staff person who will devote on-site planning and operational expertise before and during the broadcast—just as you do for the actual worship.

Local faith groups should not overlook radio and television stations when it comes to sending out news releases (see chapter three for more information on preparing news releases). For example, televisions stations often air a community calendar of upcoming non-profit, family-oriented events. Such calendars usually are brief listings of community activities aired within the local newscast. As for radio, news placement opportunities have decreased over the years as local stations have reduced their staff and air time and subscribed to national audio-feed news services and pre-packaged newscasts from news program providers. According to Vivian, fewer stations today offer news, and news-talk stations "are really more talk than news."[10]

However, not every news story works on radio or television. For television, news stories with action are more likely to get placed (e.g., a worship service that includes a lot of movements such as liturgical dance or bike-a-thon raising money to end world hunger).

Local radio and television talk shows also may provide an opportunity for faith groups to discuss important community issues or publicize their special events. Writing in *Public Relations Strategies and Tactics*, Wilcox, Ault, Agee and Cameron note some shows that are news or issues-oriented may be produced by the station's news director while other programs that are more entertainment-oriented may be produced by the program director with the help of a staff producer. Before soliciting a guest appearance on a station, faith groups should be familiar with the programs the station airs, the types of guests who have appeared on the shows, and the nature and size of the station's audience. As Wilcox et al. explain, if the station seems to be a suitable forum, then the faith group should send a one-page letter to the appropriate station personnel simply stating "whom you're offering, what their experience is, exactly what the topic would be, what shows [if any] they've been on previously, a biographical statement … as well as copies of articles on the person or topic."[11]

Outdoor and Transit

You are constantly bombarded with advertising. You try to escape by turning off the television or radio; you turn the newspaper or magazine page and ignore the message. When you leave home, you receive advertising bytes whether you want to or not. You're driving down the street and a stoplight halts the traffic. What is around you? A billboard to your right, an ad on the bus-stop bench or even larger posters inside a bus-stop shelter. The bus beside you carries an advertisement, and so does the cab in front of you.

Billboards—big, little, medium-sized—you look at them, and in four to six seconds, your brain registers their messages even if you don't consciously decide to read them. What is more, they work!

Have you thought about putting your faith message in public places? In the long run, billboards or other "out-of-home" vehicles may be the most impressive public medium a faith group can buy.

There are at least a dozen basic forms of out-of-home advertising. Different-sized billboards and posters meet different purposes. Bulletin boards are those huge billboards (14 feet high by 48 feet wide) on highways and heavily traveled streets. In most cases, they are rented from 2 to 24 months, with prices ranging from $2,000 to $30,000 per month. A "30-sheet" poster is generally used for one month. The most common size is 9 feet, 7 inches high by 21 feet, 7 inches wide. These are usually situated off of main routes of travel. Eight-sheet posters are often used with hard-to-reach and ethnic audiences. These are generally 5 feet by 11 feet. A faith group with adequate property might find that such a billboard, mounted on wheels, would grab attention in a community.

For special cases, consider these other forms of out-of-home advertising:
- commuter trains and subway displays, in passenger cars, and on station platforms;
- bus displays, exterior or interior;
- terminal displays in airports or bus stations, including diorama/islands, and ads on clocks;
- bus shelter displays for auto and pedestrian exposure;
- shopping mall displays (backlit kiosks);
- taxi displays;

- telephone enclosures, posters on public phone displays;

- painted walls (can be several stories high);

- truck displays (on side panels);

- airplane tow banners; and

- spectaculars (flashing lights and moving parts).

The displays listed above might be more useful to particular ministries, like counseling, rather than to the faith group in general.

There are drawbacks to using billboards. They are expensive when compared with newspaper ads. They are better as reminders of something the public already knows than as introductions to something new. As television, poster production can be expensive, and it has a short lifetime unless the budget can be stretched for more than one month.

However, if you are involved in several different kinds of promotion, the billboard stays up while your radio or television spots receive sporadic play. Remember that more people will see your billboard than read it in a newspaper, hear it on a radio or see it on television. Television is glamorous; radio is alluring; newspapers offer vast coverage if readers see your ad. But you may find that you get better results with out-of-home advertising than with any other medium.

Out-of-home advertising is not cheap. You may decide on less expensive media. If however, 1) your faith group provides adequate funding for communications, or 2) members are willing to provide outdoor advertising expertise and/or space, and 3) you are located in a growing area with heavy traffic, a well-placed billboard is a must.

There are several things you must do before you talk to an advertising agency or billboard company about purchasing space.

You must first determine the purpose of your advertising. Is this program meant to give your group visibility? If so, why do you want it? Is it meant to attract new members? Or is it meant to make your present fellowship feel good about itself? All are acceptable goals. However, the kind of advertising you do for visibility is different from that of attracting new members.

"Feel Good" messages make our own faith group happy to see its name in public. "Join Us" messages invite new members or participants. Your "We Can Help" group wants to reach people who need help. Identify your audience and determine why you want your message to accomplish. This is the hardest part of any campaign.

A good example of visibility and "feel good" promotion is "Catch the Spirit," created by Tennessee United Methodists in the 1980s. They wanted to tell people that United Methodists are in ministry in every community in middle Tennessee. Assisted by an advertising agency, they created newspaper slicks, bumper stickers and radio ads with a "catchy" tune, and placed 42 billboards throughout the area. The billboard was colorful, easy to read, and the message was simple. The campaign was later adopted by the entire denomination.

If your faith group is contemplating outdoor advertising, ride around and look at billboards. What makes a good billboard? First, it must be simple—the rule of thumb is no more than seven words. Your sign may read simply, "Welcome to Congregation Beth Israel," with your denominational logo, and the street address. It may be a message about special help your faith group offers, with a name and telephone number. A billboard message should be simple, brief, coherent, and as colorful as possible, so it has impact on passers-by and is easily recalled.

Color is important. People will look at a brightly colored billboard every time. Make the letter size as large as possible.

You want to catch the driver's eye, but not cause a wreck. Some billboards give a lot of detail, but unless you are parked beside them, you cannot read them. If you must have detail, put your message on a billboard beside a stop sign. However, these signs command top dollars, and are seldom available to budget-minded faith groups.

Sometimes humor is a help, but people will get tired of reading the same line each day. One denomination had a slogan that was funny the first few times: "Sundays are for sinners; come on in with the rest of us." This copy, followed by a brief invitation, made a good message for a newspaper ad but soon became irritating as a billboard message.

As you build your budget, you need to overcome two common misconceptions. The first is that members of your faith group are pleased to donate all their professional services. Even a modest reimbursement gets them to pay better attention to your program. If they want to contribute services, accept it with appropriate thanks.

The second misconception is that non-profit organizations get financial breaks from media companies. One large city billboard executive said, "Today, it seems as if everybody is non-profit. We treat them—churches, hospitals, charities—all alike—as if they are businesses. We have chosen the city zoo for our pro-bono work, and that way, we don't have to make choices about who gets discounts and who does not." An executive from a company dealing in smaller cities expressed the same idea, but said it never hurts to ask. Don't build your budget around perceived discounts.

How do you take your ideas and turn them into real billboards? The easiest way is to go to an advertising agency. An agency generally has artists and designers to make your ideas come to life in all media. It can help you record music or offer you choices from the files, for radio and television spots. The agency might be able to get you better prices and more coverage than you would be able to go yourself. However, your budget will have to be divided between paying the agency for its services and paying the media companies.

If your faith group is handling its own advertising, you can deal directly with a billboard company. Prepare by asking yourself these questions:

- Do you want your message to be seen on an interstate or local highway?
- Do you want it to be seen on primary streets close to your building?
- Do you want to target the people in certain neighborhoods?

If you are handling your own advertising, then take note of billboards locations you like, and meet with the company that owns them. Take your plans with you along with sketches of possible logos, photos and your budget.

An advertising agency will help you create ads for every medium you use, and then place them for you. The account executive will talk to you about "Showings," the various sized packages that the company offers (applies to 30-sheet posters only). Showings are measured in Gross Rating

Points (GRP). If your ad appeared on enough billboards to have #100 daily GRP/Showing, 100 percent of the population saw your ad that day, or 25 percent of the population passed your ad four times in one day, or some such combination. To attain an efficient "reach and frequency" level, you should buy no less than a #25 GRP/Showing in any single market per month. The higher the percentage of exposure, the more billboards required, the better the locations, and the higher the costs.

Prices differ in each part of the country. What you can buy in Nashville, Portland, or Omaha for $20,000 cannot be bought in major metropolitan areas such as New York, Boston, Chicago, Dallas, and Miami.

You can get more boards for your money if you are willing to be off the beaten paths. However, they will be low on the GRP/Showing range, and you may be wasting your money. Lay out your budget before your chosen billboard company, and tell them what you want—the best exposure you can get. You still won't be able to get the best locations, but you may find that at least one of your ads gets on a major thoroughfare.

When you contract with an outdoor advertising company, probably for a month, you are likely to get several services that will be helpful. Most companies have a person or department handling creativity. This person will work with you to make your idea come to life, and if the company has a graphic arts department, it will create a design for you. If not, the company will help you find someone who will handle all the production steps for your faith group. Outdoor companies will also post existing preprinted outdoor posters you may have purchased from other sources.

Online

Advertising and marketing opportunities abound on the World Wide Web. The bulk of these opportunities are being used by commercial entities. The primary method of online advertising, using advertising in its truest sense, comes in banner ads—ads that run across the top of Web pages. These ads can promote something, but they can also contain hypertext links to the Web site of the promoter. For information on Web sites and other uses of the Internet, see chapter nine.

A Final Note

One final note on advertising–in *The media of Mass Communication: 2003 Update*, John Vivian notes that the Roman Catholic Church's Pontifical Council for Social Communications handbook, Ethics in Advertising (1997), provides some helpful guidelines for those who create ads and for communicators in general. The 37-page text particularly notes the potential abuses—and harm to society—communicators should avoid as they craft advertising and other material for the media. The book notes both "the socially harmful aspects" and the "significant potential for good" that advertising and other forms of communication have and counsels communicators: "The media of social communications have two options and only two. Either they help human persons to grow in their understanding and practice of what is true and good, or they are destructive forces in conflict with human well being."[12]

Direct Mail

When was the last time you responded to something you received in the mail? What did the direct mail piece look like? Was it a catalog? A fund-raising letter? A coupon book? What is it about that piece of mail that caused you to respond? Did you like the offer? Did you like the photo? Were you interested even before opening the envelope because of the message on the front?

Most other forms of communication do not offer the control and lasting impression as inexpensively as does direct mail. Nor do they persuade as effectively as does direct mail. A direct mail piece is a good complement to an integrated communication campaign. The major drawback to direct mail is the perception that direct mail is junk mail.

The direct mail piece should stand out from other mail and invite the recipient to open it. Direct mail pieces are as individual as the products or services they promote. To help determine the appropriate type of direct mail piece, look at the product or service. What about this product is important to communicate to the customer? How can this best be accomplished? For example, if your goal is to get customers to order your video about racism, tell her in a letter how the video will benefit her, and include an easy-to-use order form and a postage-paid reply mailer. If you would like people in the neighborhood surrounding your place of worship to attend a special musical service, send out special invitations and free "tickets" that indicate when and where the concert will be held.

Direct mail is usually used to persuade or to provide information. In most cases direct mail is a sales call delivered by the post office. You are replacing a phone or personal call, not a television commercial. Normally you expect the recipient to act upon receipt of the mail. The most common means for assisting that action are the telephone and the order form.

To begin the process, ask yourself the following three questions to determine your goal for each direct mail piece.

- To whom am I speaking?
- What does the person think about my product or service now?
- What do I want the person to think?

Once you have answered these questions and formulated the answers into a goal, write it down. Look at it often as you create your direct mail campaign. Don't stray from this goal.

How do you write the copy for your direct mail piece? Generally, the fewer the words the better. However, make sure you use enough words to accomplish your goal. If you want to get people to attend your holiday service, don't just tell them when and where it is. Tell them why they should come. Always tell your audience what is in it for them. Highlight the benefits, not the features.

Asking a question is a great way to get the reader involved. Be warm and personal. Make sure the copy is "you" oriented. Using a P.S. at the bottom of a letter is a great attention-getter. People usually start with the head of a letter, read the first couple of lines, and then check to see who signed it. That's when your P.S. will grab them. Make sure you include your most valuable benefit here.

As for the actual "look" of a particular piece: generally, the more color (within reason), the greater the response (and cost). If you are using a letter, underline important points. If you are mailing in an envelope, include an important benefit statement on the front of the envelope. Don't overdo the graphics and art work at the expense of clarity.

The most important thing to remember when designing a response form is to keep it simple. A poorly designed, difficult-to-use form will cost you many valuable respondents. Look at order forms you use when ordering through the mail. Take the best things of ones you like and incorporate them into your response form. Allow ample room for respondents to write. Make sure the form includes the name and address of your faith group and a phone number or an e-mail address so people can receive additional information. You might also ask the respondent for additional names of people who might want the same information.

Who do you target with direct mail pieces? Ask yourself, "What are the characteristics of the person who needs this product or service?" Check the yellow pages of your telephone phone book under "Mailing Lists." You may also rent lists from various publications.

Interns

Faith groups should consider partnering with local colleges and universities that have academic programs in communication and are willing to place student interns with community organizations. Internships are "win-win" situations that provide much needed staffing to non-profit groups and hands-on experience for students. Interns may work on a semester or summer basis, either as volunteers or for college credit (check your legal requirements for insurance purposes), or just simply help with special projects as needed. Whether pro bono or for credit, internships should be structured so that students understand in advance what the job requires and the schedule they are to keep. Internships also should be supervised so that students receive regular feedback on their job performance. As much as possible, interns should be given meaningful assignments and not just clerical tasks. In ideal situations, an internship can become an ongoing part-time or full-time position that ultimately benefits both the faith group and student.

Resources

Advertising and Public Relations Law, by Moore, Roy L., Farrar, Ronald T., and Collins, Erik L. Mahwah, N.Y.: Lawrence Erlbaum Associates, Inc., 1997.

Advertising and the World Wide Web, by Schumann, David W. and Thorson, Esther (editors). Mahwah, N.Y.: Lawrence Erlbaum Associates, Inc., 1999.

Effective Advertising: Understanding When, How, and Why Advertising Works, by Tellis, Gerard J. Thousand Oaks, Calif.: Sage Publications, Inc., 2003.

Just a Click Away: Advertising on the Internet, by Kaye, Barbara K. and Medoff, Norman J. New York, N.Y.: Longman, 2001.

The Media Handbook: A Complete Guide to Advertising Media Selection, Planning, Research, and Buying, by Katz, Helen. Mahwah, N.Y.: Lawrence Erlbaum Associates, Inc., 2003 (second edition).

The Media of Mass Communication: 2003 Update, by Vivian, John. Boston: Allyn & Bacon, 2003 (sixth edition).

Station's Goal: Give Workers News, A Voice, by Brand, Richard. *The Miami Herald* (December 7, 2003), p. 1B.

Understanding Consumer Decision Making: The Means-End Approach to Marketing and Advertising Strategy, by Reynolds, Thomas J. and Olson, Jerry C. (editors). Mahwah, N.Y.: Lawrence Erlbaum Associates, Inc., 2001.

Using Qualitative Research in Advertising: Strategies, Techniques, and Applications, by Morrison, Margaret A., Haley, Eric, Sheehan, Kim Bartel, and Taylor, Ronald E. Thousand Oaks, Calif.: Sage Publications, Inc., 2002.

Final Thoughts

There's a divinity that shapes our ends,
Rough-hew them how we will.

—*Hamlet*, William Shakespeare

When all is said and done, religious communicators should use every means available to reach out in faith to others. As new technologies emerge, faith groups must take advantage of their particular usefulness as communication media. As the Most Reverend Robert F. Morneau noted in *St. Anthony Messenger*, "Would not St. Paul, if alive today, be on television and sending out epistles via the Internet?"[13]

Faith groups, of course, have a special purpose—or calling—that directs their communication efforts. And that mission ultimately should shape not only the content and direction but the very nature of such communication. Whether reaching out within their communities or to those outside, religious communicators must always model the very highest of ethical standards in their work. The "word enfleshed" in print, on radio or television, or over the Internet, should reflect a faith community's concern for truth, human dignity, and social responsibility. We can and should do no less.

Ultimately, though, it will be our actions that either confirm or deny our words however well they are communicated. As religious communicators, we must not only "mean what we say" and "say what we mean" but "do what we say." In the final analysis, it will be in the doing that our integrity will be measured. And, in acting rightly, we may find the truest and best way in which to communicate. As St. Francis of Assisi once said, "Be special. You may be the only Gospel your neighbor will ever read."

ENDNOTES

1 *Saintly Campaigning: Devotional-Promotional Communication and the U.S. Tour of St. Therese's Relic*, by Tilson, Donn James and Chao, Yi-Yuan. Journal of Media and Religion (Vol. 1, Number 2, 2002), pp. 81-104.

2 *When Your Client is God*, by Randall, Virginia. PRWeek (March 13, 2000), pp. 20-21.

3 *Power-Packed PR: Ideas That Work*, by Fulginiti, Anthony J. Pitman: New Jersey: Communication Publications and Resources, 1988.

4 Religious Tourism, Public Relations and Church-State Partnerships, by Donn James Tilson. *Public Relations Quarterly* (Fall 2001), pp. 35-39.

5 *The Media of Mass Communication: 2003 Update*, by Vivian, John. Boston: Allyn & Bacon, 2003 (sixth edition).

6 Ibid

7 Ibid

8 *Proposal for a Catholic Radio Station*, by Tobin, Richard W., and Tilson, Donn J.. Miami: Archdiocese of Miami Communications Commission, 1989

9 Station's Goal: Give Workers News, A Voice, by Brand, Richard. *The Miami Herald* (December 7, 2003), p. 1B.

10 Vivian, op.cit.

11 *Public Relations Strategies and Tactics*, by Wilcox, D.L., Ault, P.H., Agee, W., and Cameron, G.T. New York, N.Y.: Longman, 2003 (seventh edition).

12 Vivian, op.cit.

13 *Spirituality for the New Millennium*, by Morneau, R. St. Anthony Messenger (August 2000), pp. 12-16

III. We've Got the Whole World in Our Hands:
Communicating in the Larger Community

Chapter 13

We've Got a Situation Here:
Crisis Communication

By Daniel R. Gangler

Boston religion news rocked when the Roman Catholic Church was tried both in the courts and in the media for the sexual abuse of several priests against boys over a 20-year time period. *The Boston Globe* carried more than 600 stories during the crisis. All broadcast and cable news media carried the story for weeks.

As a result of the crisis, Pope John Paul reassigned the archbishop and gave new leadership to the two million-member archdiocese. This was a crisis for the Catholic Church in Boston, but it also spilled over into other cities and other faith groups as well, as the general public scrutinized the conduct of clergy. On his July 2003 installation as the new archbishop of Boston, the Most Reverend Seán Patrick O'Malley, said: "How we ultimately deal with the present crisis in our church will do much to define us as Catholics of the future."

From the viewpoint of a communicator, crisis has been defined in several ways. One definition comes from William N. Curry, at the Public Relations Society of America National Conference in 1997 when he said: "Crisis is a situation that puts your organization's values on trial in the court of public opinion."

This definition separates crisis from disaster. Disaster happens to the general population or an entire geographic area and each organization reacts to disaster in a variety of ways. Hurricanes, tornadoes, volcanic eruptions are examples of natural disasters. The Sept. 11, 2001 destruction of the World Trade Center towers and the Oklahoma City bombing in April 1995 are examples of man-made disasters.

- Crisis challenges and changes an organization.
- Crisis stimulates media coverage.
- Crisis becomes a pivotal point for the way organizations operate in the future.
- Crisis ripples beyond an organization into the lives of families and community.
- Crisis can be good and bad in the life of an organization. Scandals and tremendous rapid growth of a faith community can each evoke a crisis.

Whatever the event or series of events that causes crisis, an organization's managers, legal consultants and communicators must work together in a coordinated and integrated way to live through the crisis with minimum damage to the organization and its values.

In the second or 1999 edition of *Not If, But When*, Alan Griggs, then director of media strategy for United Methodist Communications, outlines five common components of a crisis.

1. **Crises usually come suddenly.** Many times they catch us by surprise. We need a plan of action before a crisis arises.

2. **Adequate information and key leaders are not always available at a time of a crisis.** Griggs writes, "Remember this rule of thumb: the news is biggest when the facts are fewest." And without facts, accusations, speculations, and suspicions abound. We need a plan of action.

3. **Every crisis provides its own opportunity—early—to position the organization as it would like to be understood.** We need a plan of action. When crisis occurs, according to Curry, the public expects the organization to:

   - Care about what happened.

   - Do something about the crisis.

   - Tell how it will prevent a recurrence.

4. **Each crisis has a life cycle.**
   - Warnings.

   - The crisis event.

   - An investigation.

   - A determination of how the organization will resolve the crisis so it doesn't happen again.

   If a crisis is not resolved, it will occur again. A crisis just doesn't go away over time. We need a plan of action.

5. **All crises tend to impair judgment and clear thinking.** Crises put us on the defensive. We need to take an offensive approach. We need to check hostility. We need to remember, everything is on the record even in private when dealing with a crisis. Ill chosen words and actions can escalate a crisis. We need a plan of action.

Take a few moments and list the crises that have and could happen to your organization. Rank them as personal and institutional.

Personal Crises:
- Religious leader accused of sexual misconduct.

- Religious leader diagnosed with HIV and refuses to resign.

- Leader killed in automobile accident on a youth retreat.

- Music director accused of sexual misconduct by choir member.

- Student raped in residence hall on campus of a faith-related university.

Institutional crises:
- Confidential information disclosed.

- Dismissed employee charges age discrimination.

- Several parents allege sexual misconduct in pre-school.

- Treasurer disappears and so do several thousands of dollars.

- Bomb threat issued to daycare program.

- Overseas relief worker reported killed by terrorist.

- Threatening letters sent to faith community leader.

A wise communication program will plan for a crisis. Sooner or later, a crisis will come and communicators need to be ready.

Recruit a Crisis Communication Team

Even though no one knows what will be the next crisis or when it will happen, you can prepare for crisis by building a team to communicate to public media, to your membership, and to neighboring communities.

> **Build two teams.**
> A primary or permanent team needs to include: the chief executive officer or executive officer of the congregation such as a pastor, priest, or rabbi; communication officer; and president of the congregation or chair of the congregation's administrative council.
>
> A secondary or supportive team could include: legal counsel, supervisory representative of the regional faith group, treasurer, possibly a representative from a public relations firm, and a secretary or administrative assistant.
>
> **Each team member needs to:**
> - Be assigned a particular role and responsibility in the decision-making process.
> - Know the details of the crisis.
> - Agree on the way the crisis will be communicated.
> - Decide on a spokesperson.

The spokesperson for the organization in a time of crisis needs to be the congregation's administrative officer such as pastor, priest, or rabbi. If this person is not available, the president of the congregation or chair of the congregation's administrative council needs to assume this role.

The organization's communicator relates to the media and may be empowered to speak on behalf of the faith group; however, the communicator should always be involved deeply in the process and administration of communication during a crisis. Working with the executives and officers of an organization, it is the task of the communicator to draft news releases.

If the crisis involves the courts or local officials, legal counsel needs to be consulted to suggest and review news releases and statements to media.

Once the team is in place, a communication plan needs to follow. If your organization does not have a crisis communication plan in place, take steps now with the officers of the organization to write a communication plan so that it can be approved and implemented when needed. We don't organize a fire department to take care of a fire, we call 911 and the fire department is dispatched. Likewise, when a crisis strikes, we need to call the crisis communications team together, not invent it. Remember, crisis strikes rapidly and needs a response within at least two hours.

Take Action

React to the crisis in an open, direct, accurate and truthful manner. Respond directly to the situation in a timely manner that shows compassion and explains what measures your organization is taking to prevent the crisis from reoccurring. Prepare for interviews.

As the communications officer of an organization, when a crisis occurs, work with your superiors to put the team in place. Here are some questions that need answers to put your team into action:

- Who will speak on behalf of the organization? Where? When?

- Who will draft a statement? Remember to include in the statement: response, compassion, and prevention.

- Who will review the statement? The statement needs to be reviewed by the chief executive officer, communicator, highest elected official, and legal counsel if this crisis involves the law. Remember the larger the team, the more time it will take to have everyone review the statement. Be ready to respond to a crisis within two hours.

- Who will continue to speak for the organization. The communicator needs to take a proactive role and not wait for other leaders to act. However, he/she should always act in concert with the other leaders of the organization. Public media will seek out the communicator, but they may also try to circumvent the communicator to go directly to the chief executive officer. If the officer begins to answer questions without the communicator's knowledge, the effectiveness of the team can be damaged causing it to play a defensive role rather than taking the offensive. The team needs to keep its own lines of communication open.

Prepare the Statement

The statement needs to contain the elements of response, compassion and prevention. Write the statement out for review and stick to it as various media sources call on you for a statement. Keep the statement focused and constant. Use positive words and phrases. Tell the truth, but not everything you know. Use complete sentences. Talk to the policies and procedures, which policies have been violated, and what procedures you are talking to correct this matter.

Supplement your statement with documents concerning policies and procedures for this particular crisis. This might also be in the form or charts and graphs.

The written statement needs to be supplemented by contact information such as the name and title of the communicator, the official name of the organization, the street address, phone number, fax number, and cell phone number. Don't list the contact information of other team members. Let the communicator determine which reporter should speak with which individual. Remember that during a crisis, the role of the chief executive officer, treasurer, legal consultant, and others is something other than communication.

The Interview

Setting: If other than a telephone interview, choose the best setting for the interview. What location gives you the best control and communicates the mission of the organization? Consider these locations—your office, a conference room, a board room, the executive staff officer's office, a neutral location, a place of worship. If this is a television interview, choose the location of the crisis. Use the entrance of the location. Do not allow a camera crew to roam the interior of the location of the crisis. You choose the place and invite the media.

Rehearse: If there is time, rehearse the interview with the spokesperson. Other members of the team may ask questions to simulate an interview.

Tips for the Talk: Here are lists of "dos" and "don'ts" developed by United Methodist Communications for directors of communication.

Do:
- Open with your main point.
- Show compassion and concern.
- Use only confirmed factual information.
- Identify how the problem is being "fixed" or investigated.
- Talk with sound bites—15 seconds for radio and TV (speak with rapid pace); one to two sentences for print media (speak so you can be quoted correctly).
- Focus on policies and procedures when you cannot address the specifics.
- Remember: response, compassion, and prevention.

Don't:
- Use acronyms or inside language.
- Take questions when you don't have enough information about the crisis.
- Give your opinion.
- Show anger or get defensive.
- Repeat negatives.
- Speculate, guess or speak outside of your expertise.
- Make assumptions about innocence or guilt.
- Say "no comment."
- Speak "off the record."

The Press Conference

If you receive five or more requests for interviews, you may want to hold a press conference. Here are some things to consider:

- Inform media by e-mail and phone calls when and where the conference will be held.
- Do not release any statement until it has been read at the news conference.
- Select a location that you can control and which says something visually.
- Use an entrance area that shows this is a religious organization.
- Determine who will make the statement.
- Ask media to sign in giving names, news organization, and telephone number.
- Ask an administrative assistant to courteously restrict the press to one area.
- Set a time that is sensitive to news deadlines.
- If using a podium, display organizational logo on front of podium.
- Ask an assistant to distribute materials and take notes on the conference.
- Distribute news releases, supporting documents, and fact sheet about organization.
- Begin on time with words of compassion if not contained in statement.
- The statement can contain a quote from the chief executive officer.
- Read statement.
- Use confirmed facts.
- Keep statement and responses to questions short and direct.
- Refer to policy and procedures.
- Don't speculate. Say "I don't know. I can check on that."
- Speak slowly, confidently and naturally.
- Make eye contact with reporters; don't look into cameras.
- End questions when you choose to end conference.
- Summarize by repeating statements of response, compassion, and prevention.
- Let media know when you will speak with them again.

Review: Ask your crisis communication team to review the conference as soon as reporters have left.

- What went well?
- What needs improvement?

Conclusion

Conclude an interview or press conference with contact information including name, title, organization and where you can be reached. Let the reporter know that you are open to further questions at another time. You may need to research information requested and return a call to the reporter. Do this a quickly as possible. Ask the reporter for his or her contact information or business card. Ask the reporter what his or her deadline is and try to respect that deadline. Remember that the words, "The spokesperson could not be reached for comment," or "The spokesperson did not provide requested information" can work against your communication efforts.

A Communicator Tells His Story

The father of a family systematically killed his wife, children and himself over a two-day period. Unknown to many, he was deeply in debt.

When I heard a radio news story, I contacted the senior pastor letting him know that he would face a communication crisis when the media found out that all the family were members of his congregation. We assumed this information would become public when funeral arrangements were announced. This gave just enough time for the pastor and me to establish a communication plan.

The deceased wife's family did not want a public memorial service. Since these tragic deaths affected hundreds of people in the community including school children, teachers, professional colleagues, and the members of the congregation, the pastor convinced both families that a community memorial service was necessary for the mourning of the community.

Once the media heard about the memorial service, they wanted full coverage of the service with cameras and tape recorders. I advised the pastor to provide alternatives to the media's requests and to keep the coverage controlled.

The pastor held a press briefing for television and radio media before the memorial service. The briefing was held on the church steps. Newspaper and radio media were asked not to bring cameras or personal recorders into the sanctuary, but reporters were invited to attend the public service. Since the church had a radio ministry, the service was recorded and reporters requesting a recording of the service were given one immediately after the service.

Following the memorial service, the pastor was available to the media for personal and telephone interviews. He confined his answers to spiritual concerns. Private funeral services were held for family members on another day.

The tragic deaths of this family brought a crisis to this congregation. But instead of shutting the media out, the leaders of the congregation found ways to assist the media in covering their stories while maintaining the sanctity of a public memorial service.

Chapter 14

America Is Interfaith

By Anuttama Dasa

> **The radicalism of religious diversity is a fact of contemporary life and may well become the most significant feature in the development of society and culture in the twenty-first century.**
>
> **—*The Culture of Religious Pluralism*, Richard E. Wentz**[1]

Life in America is an interfaith experience. In my own life, my doctor is Hindu. My Vietnamese barber is Catholic, my acupuncturist is a Taiwanese Buddhist, my next-door neighbors are Sikh, my UPS driver is a Baptist youth minister, my chiropractor is Jewish, and one of my employees is Muslim.

Atypical? Not necessarily. According to Harvard University's Pluralism Project, in addition to an abundance of Protestant denominations and Roman Catholic orders, in America today there are approximately 6 million Muslims, 6 million Jews, 3 million Buddhists, 1 million Hindus, 250,000 Sikhs, and 150,000 Baha'is. That's a fair amount of diversity—and the numbers are increasing.

Two important questions arise: While we are certainly a diverse group of citizens, do we know each other? And, should religious organizations strive to promote understanding and cooperation among the people of various faiths that call themselves Americans?

Seeing the Other

It is a broad-minded person who doesn't feel uncomfortable with, if not threatened by, the wide array of religious expression we encounter in our lives. Scholars analyze several different categories of response to these diverse versions of truth. Julia Mitchell Corbett, of Ball State University, denotes five:

> **Exclusivism** holds that "because religion deals with ultimate truth, there can only be one true or correct religion, and the rest are simply wrong...."

> **Relativism** maintains that "all perspectives are limited, even those that lay claim to absolute truth...[therefore] religions are all wrong and none is worthy of one's commitment...[or] in the absence of knowable absolute truth, the choice of a religion is simply up to individuals to pick the religion that feels right for them...."

> **Inclusivism** holds that "there is one true or best religion, one that holds within itself the fullness of religious truth and human salvation. However, there is something of this truth in some other religions, as well...."

> **Synthesis** believes that "all religions are essentially the same underneath a veneer of cultural particularity. The differences among the religions are downplayed in favor of the similarities among them. Thus, all will—or at least should—come together into a unity...."

Affirmation or pluralism holds that "the different religions are simply different, not headed towards a synthesis and not subsumable under [a] big umbrella...each is ultimately true [at least in the eyes of its followers] and must be honored as such...."[2]

Whatever our perspective on the religious "other," whenever we meet our child's new Buddhist friend, attend a PTA meeting led by a Christian Scientist, or sit near an Orthodox rabbi on the bus, we experience an interfaith world. Want to speak of the broader context of our ever-shrinking global village? International conditions compel us to acknowledge and learn to peacefully coexist with the richly diverse, yet often conflicting worldviews that share our planet.

Land of the Free

America is a nation that prides itself on diversity and the guarantee of liberty for all citizens. Our children are taught from their earliest years that America was founded on the principle of religious freedom. The first Europeans came here with the desire to serve God according to the dictations of their hearts, free from the dictations of the state. The early pilgrims, and millions who followed them, came to the New World to escape religious oppression.

Yet, despite this ideal, the history of religious freedom in the United States is not without blemish. Roger Williams fled Massachusetts and sought refuge in the wilderness of Rhode Island where he could practice his Baptist faith undisturbed. Native Americans suffered religious bigotry and ethnic genocide. Members of the Latter-Day Saints were driven from New York to Illinois and finally to the shore of the Great Salt Lake before they found shelter from religious persecution. Jews and Catholics have faced great prejudice and discrimination, as have, in different times and places, devout Protestants.

Why is this history important to us? Because as religion communicators we are painfully aware that "religious people" are often the most vigorous in persecuting others. All too often the persecution of one faith was, and is, perpetrated by members of another.

As people of faith, we realize that to preserve our own freedoms, we need to protect the freedoms of the minorities among us. And, in an ever expanding global context, we realize that no matter what our faith tradition may be, there will always be somewhere in the world where our members are the minority.

Guidelines for Meeting People of another Faith

Simply put, the basic ingredient of an interfaith exchange is when two or more people of different faith traditions meet. The National Council of Churches highlights five essential features of an open and fruitful relationship with a person of another faith:

"True relationship involves risk. When we approach others with an open heart, it is possible that we may be hurt. When we encounter others with an open mind, we may have to change our positions or give up certainty, but we may gain new insights...."

"True relationship respects the other's identity. We will meet others as they are, in their particular hopes, ideas, struggles and joys. These are articulated through their own traditions, practices and world-views...."

"True relationship is based on integrity. If we meet others as they are, then we must accept their right to determine and define their own identity. We also must remain faithful to who we are...We will not ask others to betray their religious commitments...nor will we betray our commitment...."

"True relationship is rooted in accountability and respect. We approach others in humility, not arrogance. In our relationships we will call ourselves and our partners to a mutual accountability. We will invite each other to join in building a world of love and justice, but we will also challenge each other's unjust behavior. We can do both only from an attitude of mutual respect...."

"True relationship offers an opportunity to serve... we will join with those of other religious traditions to serve the whole of God's creation...."[3]

Dialogue

A notable method of interface between people of different faiths is dialogue. The National Conference for Community and Justice offers this definition:

"Dialogue is a process through which people share openly and honestly their views, attitudes, beliefs and feelings about a subject. The goal of dialogue is both simple and complex: to deepen and widen our understanding of ourselves and those with whom we dialogue."

"Genuine dialogue implies the possibility of being changed by the experience; therefore, dialogue is inherently risky! For true dialogue to occur, participants must have a safe environment of mutually accepted rights and responsibilities. These rights and responsibilities are rooted in two fundamental values: respect for the other person and trust in the benefits of dialogue."[4]

Forms of Dialogue

Ecumenical dialogue is between different denominations of Christians, for instance Methodists and Episcopalians. Interfaith dialogue, or inter-religious dialogue, is between people different religions, for example Roman Catholics and Buddhists, or Hindus and Muslims.

Dialogue can be formal or informal. It can range from a conversation between passersby on the street questioning each other's religious garb, to an international conference at the United Nations. Whatever the size and scope, scholars note that interfaith dialogue—and interfaith organizations—generally have three or four varieties of focus. Father Thomas Ryan, director of the Paulist Office for Ecumenical and Interfaith Relations, describes these as follows:

> "The dialogue of life where people strive to live in an open and neighborly spirit, sharing their joys and sorrows, their human preoccupations and problems; a focus on practical shared service to humanity."

> "The dialogue of action, in which Christians and others collaborate for the integral development and liberation of people."

> "The dialogue of theological exchange, where specialists seek to deepen their understanding of their respective heritages and appreciate each other's spiritual values, always bearing in mind the need to search for the ultimate truth"

> "The dialogue of religious experience, in which persons, rooted in their own religious traditions, share their spiritual riches, for instance with regard to prayer and contemplation."

Some interfaith groups, for example, forge common strategies to address poverty or racism. Others focus on building understanding between different viewpoints, thus seeking to increase appreciation of our shared humanity and to minimize conflict. Still others provide participants with an experience of each other's practice and spirituality.

Why Interfaith?

"We come together because our love for God and humanity inspires it; our concern for justice, freedom and peace demands it; and what we can learn from each other requires it. Baha'i, Hindu, Islamic, Jewish, Latter-day Saints, Protestant, Roman Catholic, Sikh and Zoroastrian, through our collaboration in the Interfaith Conference we intend to be a symbol of moral unity in a broken world."

—Vision Statement of the Interfaith Conference of Metropolitan Washington, D.C.

"Because God is at work in all creation, we can expect to find new understanding of our faith through dialogue with people of other religions. Such interaction can be an opportunity for mutual witness..."

**—"Interfaith Relations and the Churches,"
A Policy Statement of the National Council of Churches of Christ in the U.S.A., Article 28**

"Various documents of the Second Vatican Council (1962-5) recognize that there exist in other religious traditions 'elements which are true and good,' 'precious things, both religious and human,' 'seeds of contemplation,' 'elements of truth and grace,' 'seeds of the Word' and 'rays of truth which illumine all humankind.' These values merit the attention and the esteem of Christians. Their spiritual patrimony is a genuine invitation to dialogue, not only in those things which unite us, but also in our differences."

—From the Paulist Fathers Web site: www.paulist.org/mission/ecumenism.html

"We can no longer afford relations that barely exist. The Union [of Reform Judaism] has joined with four Christian denominations in calling for dialogue...Congregations are asked to join with a church in the community and...come together to learn about common aspects of our history and about critical distinctions..."

—From the Union of Reform Judaism Web site: www.urj.org/opendoors/

"The Qur'an, which the Muslims believe is the revelation of God given to the Prophet Muhammad, recognizes the universal moral norms that touch all human beings even when they follow their particular 'revealed' paths. Moreover, these universally objective values are 'ingrained in human soul' (91.8) in the form of nature, which transcends different religions and religious communities."

**—Abdulaziz Sachedina, "Universal and Particular Discourse in
the Islamic Tradition A Muslim Response," in Learning to Dialogue,
Building Interreligious Community, Church and Society, Sept/Oct. 1992**

"As people of faith, we hold more in common than we are accustomed to acknowledging. The work of interfaith dialogue is to explore these areas and to build on them. And once we have built these bridges of understanding, it will be easier to explore the points of difference."

—Richard Landau, "What the World Needs to Know About Interfaith Dialogue," (Baha'i)
www.interfaithdialog.org/Articles/Landau.pdf

Fools Rush in where Angels Dare Not Tread

Many of us in the religious community are inspired to share our beliefs and spread our mission. Keep in mind, however, an interfaith dialogue is not the place to seek converts. When in dialogue with members of another tradition, the goal is to learn and to build positive, mutually beneficial relationships—not to win over the other side. The critical skill here is listening. By divine plan we are all blessed with two ears and one mouth. It's important to note that while our ears are designed to be open twenty-four hours a day, the default position for our mouth is closed. We might well ask, "What is God telling us about the value of listening?"

Caution in our use of language is also important. Words commonly used by one faith may appear exclusive, or even offensive, to another. In an interfaith environment, we need to be sensitive to the language we use and be as inclusive as possible. It may be better, for example, to speak of "houses of worship" or "community of faith" rather than "churches;" better to speak of different "religious traditions" rather than "denominations;" better to address the "Creator God," the "Supreme Truth," or the "Source of all Being," rather than use terms unique to our tradition. In prayer, it may be appropriate to end with "we ask this in your name," or "please hear our prayer."

Actually, there are two schools of thought here. In some interfaith circles, offered prayers are required to contain broad language that embrace as many faiths as possible. Specific prayers dear to a given tradition are often put aside out of fear of exclusivity. However, it's also true that while generic language avoids the offensive, it may expunge the essential. It is the unique expression of faith and imagery that evokes the richness of a spiritual tradition.

One possible solution is for interfaith sessions to begin with prayers or scriptural readings from a variety of traditions. Thus, no one need stretch their vocabulary to offer a prayer inclusive of all the faiths present. The audience understands that each particular reading reflects the values of a specific belief. Of course, in all circumstances the prayers we choose should avoid language that is clearly exclusive, appears to proselytize, or is disrespectful.

Rights, Risks and Responsibilities of Dialogue

The National Conference for Community and Justice (NCCJ) recommends the following rights and responsibilities for dialogue. Participants in a NCCJ dialogue read these principles together as a prerequisite before every session and must sign an agreement to abide by them. This is an excellent tool to assure a collegial mood. Occasional mid-session reference to this list is also effective in keeping a group on track and minimizing conflict or abrasiveness.

We believe that true dialogue can occur when all participants honor at least the following rights and responsibilities:

The right to:
- Express his or her beliefs, ideas and feelings.
- Define him/herself without being labeled by others.
- Ask questions that help him/her understand what someone is saying.
- Not change or be forced to change.
- Ask others to hold what he or she says in confidence.

Each person has the responsibility to:
- Listen to others patiently and without judgment.
- Not make untested assumptions about others.
- Answer questions in ways that help others understand him or her.
- Grant basic respect to others, even in conflict or disagreement.
- Hold in confidence what others say.
- Be continually present and attentive to the process.

—Reprinted with permission

Diet

Many religions have dietary restrictions. Muslims abstain from pork and fast from sunrise to sunset during the month of Ramadan. Many Jews observe kosher guides. Jains, as well as most Hindus, Seventh-Day Adventists, and some Buddhists, are vegetarians. Among vegetarians, some not only avoid meat, fish, and eggs but also dairy products.

When catering an interfaith event, it is often essential to provide vegetarian options. It is best to ask participants ahead of time if they have any special dietary needs. Many interfaith groups, out of respect for the vegetarians, provide only meatless meals. Some are careful to offer vegetarian selections from a separate serving table.

Similarly, many religions abstain from alcohol. Strict Methodists, Muslims, Mormons, Vaishnavas and others would be disturbed if the only punch available—had a punch.

Interfaith Options

Over the last few years the number of interfaith meetings and dialogue opportunities has increased dramatically. Chances are there is an interfaith group nearby that welcomes you and the participation of your faith community. If not, there is no better time to start one than now!

Faith leaders and lay people alike can be enthusiastic about the possibility of participating in interfaith dialogue. The World Wide Web is a limitless resource of organizations and individual religious and spiritual communities interested in dialogue. (See resources at the end of this chapter for a partial list.) Beliefnet.org provides interfaith chat rooms and dialogue sessions on line.

There are a variety of interfaith functions and structures; some are local, some national, and some international. A forum can easily be inaugurated with just a few inexpensive ingredients: An interesting theme or topic for discussion, a list of local contacts for houses of worship, a convenient and welcoming place to meet, a few refreshments, a sincere desire to build community relations, and a humble and gracious mood. Below is a list of ten popular types of interfaith meetings:

1) Interfaith religious leaders meet regularly to discuss their beliefs and share community concerns.

2) Members of your faith group, or youth group, visit different places of worship to learn about other faith communities and to make new friends.

3) Interfaith leaders meet with political leaders to discuss their perspectives on issues.

4) Interfaith groups organize lay members and religious leaders to tackle a specific social problem.

5) Friends of diverse faiths are invited to your home for an evening of shared prayers, music, chants, or readings from their respective traditions.

6) Diverse religious leaders speak and share views at an important community event.

7) Organized retreats invite people of different faiths to be together, share, and learn about one another.

8) Other religious groups are invited to visit your community and share worship services.

9) Diverse youth groups work together to clean up a river, park or participate in a social improvement project.

10) Special events such as interfaith concerts, seminars and workshops provide forums to discuss social issues, or perspectives on faith.

America is interfaith. As religion communicators, we have a special opportunity to involve our religious community, our faith leaders, and our family and friends in building interfaith relations. The world will be enriched by it—and so will we.

A Code for Interfaith Conduct

- The main aim [of dialogue] is to form genuine friendly relationships that promote understanding between our selves and members of other religions.

- Listen with respect to and value presentations by members of other faiths.

- Give members of other faiths the opportunity to freely express their sincerely held beliefs and convictions.

- Allow members of other faiths to define themselves in their own language and own culture without imposing definitions upon them, thus avoiding comparing their practice with our ideals.

- Respect the diet, dress, rituals and etiquette of others.

- Recognize that we all can fall short of the ideals of our respective traditions.

- Do not misrepresent or disparage the beliefs or religious practices of others. If you want to understand their beliefs, inquire politely and humbly.

- Respect that others have a commitment to their chosen faith as you do to yours.

- Be honest, sensitive and courteous to all you meet, even if you do not get a chance to interact on a deeper level.

- Respect the right of others to disagree and their desire to be left alone.

- There is never a need to compromise our philosophy or values.

—"ISKCON in Relation to People of Faith in God,"
ISKCON Communications Journal, Volume 7, No. 1 June, 1999,
International Society for Krishna Consciousness Interfaith
Policy Statement (Reprinted with permission)

Resources

Organizations/Web Sites

Belief Net, Media site (www.beliefnet.org)

Pluralism Project, Harvard University (www.pluralism.org)

United Religions Initiative (www.uri.org/resources)

United States Conference of Religions for Peace (www.uscrp.org)

North American Interfaith Network (www.nain.org)

National Conference for Community and Justice (www.nccj.org)

Interfaith Conference of Metropolitan D.C. (www.interfaith-metrodc.org)

International Interfaith Centre, Oxford, England (www.interfaith-center.org)

National Council of Churches of Christ (www.ncccusa.org/interfaith/ifrhome.html.)

Paulist Fathers, Roman Catholic (www.paulist.org/mission/ecumenism.html)

Books

M. Darrol Bryant and S.A. Ali, eds., *Muslim-Christian Dialogue: Promise and Problems* (St. Paul, MN: Paragon House, 1998)

Julia Mitchell Corbett, *Religion in America*, Fourth Edition (Upper Saddle River, NJ: Prentice Hall, 2000)

Diana Eck, *Encountering God: A Spiritual Journey from Bozeman to Benares* (Boston: Beacon Press, 1993)

1 Richard E. Wentz, *The Culture of Religious Pluralism* (Boulder, CO: Westview Press, 1998), p.13.

2 *Religion in America*, Fourth Edition, Julia Mitchell Corbett (Upper Saddle River, NJ: Prentice Hall 2000), p. 2-5, Excerpts

3 "Interfaith Relations and the Churches," A Policy Statement of the National Council of Churches of Christ in the U.S.A., (Nos. 48-52)

4 "Rights, Risks and Responsibilities of Dialogue," National Conference for Community and Justice (NCCJ), formerly the National Conference for Christians and Jews

5 Paulist Fathers Website,www.paulist.org/mission/ecuminism.html

Chapter 15

A Crash Course in Copyrights

Ethical Issues Related to Communications

By Rachel Riensche

Whether you've just started your communications job or you're a veteran communicator, copyright-related questions can seem confusing. If you become familiar with a few copyright basics, you'll be well quipped to handle the copyright questions that land at your desk.

What is a copyright?

A copyright is a collection of rights that belong exclusively to the copyright owner. Copyright laws are intended to encourage the creation of new material by assuring that those rights are protected.

A copyright holder has five exclusive rights. These are the right to:

- Reproduce the work.
- Prepare derivative works (works derived from the original work such as abridgments, translations or other adaptations).
- Distribute the work.
- Perform the work.
- Display the work.

Copyright protection is available for a wide range of creative work. Works of authorship that are eligible for copyright include the following categories:

- Literary works.
- Musical works, including any accompanying words.
- Dramatic works, including any accompanying music.
- Pantomimes and choreographic works.
- Pictorial, graphic, and sculptural works.
- Motion pictures and other audiovisual works.
- Sound recordings.
- Architectural works.

Regardless of the form in which it they are described, explained, illustrated, or embodied, there's no copyright protection for ideas, procedures, processes, systems, methods of operation, concepts, principles, or discoveries.

Who owns the copyright?

Initially, the copyright belongs to the author. Typically that's the person who created the work. However, if the creative work meets the requirements for a "work for hire," then the copyright belongs to the employer or the party that commissioned the work to be done.

As a valuable form of property, a copyright can be bought, sold, licensed, mortgaged, and inherited. To determine the current owner, look for the copyright notice on the publication or for a listing that acknowledges the owner of any preexisting material in the publication. If someone other than the owner administers the copyright, then that information is often included along with the statement of copyright ownership.

How does one get a copyright?

Copyright subsists in original works of authorship. If a work is eligible for copyright protection, then the owner automatically has the five exclusive rights of copyright ownership.

Provided the creative work is eligible for copyright, the author may include a copyright notice on it. Including a copyright notice on a creative work announces who owns the copyright present in that work. A copyright notice includes three elements:

- The word copyright (or the symbol "©" or abbreviation "copyr.").
- The year the work was created.
- The name of the copyright claimant.

To obtain some additional valuable legal protection, the author may wish to register the copyright with the U.S. Copyright Office. However, the author owns the copyright of a creative work even before it is registered. Filing a copyright registration is a simple procedure and assures that the owner of the copyright receives the full protection of the copyright law. Copyright registration forms are available on the US Copyright Office web site.

If there is no copyright notice, does that mean that it is not protected under copyright?

Don't assume that material is in the pubic domain if there's no copyright notice. The notice may be missing for a number of reasons, for example:

- The material is only an excerpt from a larger publication and the copyright notice is found elsewhere.
- The copyright notice was unintentionally omitted from this printing of the publication and appears in later reprints. Because recent changes in the copyright law have revised the notice requirements, it is always wise to do some research before assuming that material without a copyright notice is actually in the public domain.
- The material may be an unauthorized photocopy and the copyright notice has been intentionally omitted.

How long does a copyright last?

The length of copyright protection varies according to when the work was created. Although specific circumstances determine the exact duration of the copyright, a rule of thumb is to assume that works created:

- Prior to 1978 may be protected for 95 years.
- In 1978 or later may be protected for the author's lifetime plus 70 years.
- Works that are not protected by copyright are said to be in the "public domain."

The status of the copyright does not depend on whether a publication is in print. "Out of print" simply means that the printed copies of the publication are no longer available for purchase; the work may be protected by copyright, however. Many out-of-print publications remain protected by copyright and are not in the public domain.

Can I use copyrighted material without contacting the owner?

A copyright is a valuable form of property. Just like other forms of property, the owner or administrator has authority to allow another person to exercise any of the owner's exclusive rights.

If you're considering the using one of these exclusive rights of copyright ownership, you'll need to get permission from the copyright owner or administrator. The only exceptions are for situations that are considered a "fair use."

What is "Fair Use"?

Ordinarily, only the copyright holder may exercise any of the exclusive rights of copyright ownership. Under very limited circumstances, someone other than the copyright holder may exercise one of these rights. This appropriate use of copyrighted material without prior permission is called a "fair use."

The copyright law does not clearly define the limits of fair use, but it does list the following points that must be considered when determining if a proposed use of an exclusive right falls within the scope of a fair use:

> The purpose and character of the use. Situations where the user gains from the use of copyrighted material without paying for it are typically outside the bounds of fair use.

> The nature of the copyrighted work. Facts and other compilations of data ordinarily may be reproduced more freely than fiction, poetry, music, or other similar material.

> The amount and substantiality of the material used in relation to the copyrighted work as a whole. Even a seemingly small amount of material may represent a substantial portion of a work. For example, one stanza of a two-stanza poem represents 50 percent of a copyrighted work.

> The effect of the use on the value of the existing work. Copying may not compete with or replace the purchase of the original copyrighted use.

The copyright law also states that reproducing a copyrighted work for "criticism, comment, news reporting, teaching, scholarship, or research" is not an infringement of the copyright holder's rights. However, many situations that commonly occur in not-for-profit organizations are not eligible for a fair-use exception and their use requires permission just as they would if used by a for-profit context.

How do I request permission to use copyrighted material?

Every copyright holder determines the policies concerning the way in which a particular copyright is administered. Most copyright owners require permission requests to be made in writing. If the copyright holder is a publisher, direct your inquiry to "Copyright Permissions."

Requests are evaluated based on the information provided to the copyright owner. To speed the process, be sure to include the following:

What you want to use: Title, author or composer, pages, copyright year, ISBN or other identification number, a description of what is to be used (exact sentences, paragraphs).

How it will be used: The rights requested (one-time event, permanent publication), intended audience, number of copies to be made, selling price, format (magazine, book, event program), name and date of the event (as appropriate).

Who you are: Name, address, phone number of the organization, as well as the same information for the contact person making the request.

After your request is received and researched, you will typically receive a written response either granting permission (including the terms of the permission and any required copyright credit lines) or an explanation stating why the permission cannot be granted.

What if I don't get a reply from the copyright owner? Can I use the material?

There's always risk associated with using another person's property without their permission, and that's true for the use of copyright as well. Without a "fair use" exception to authorize your use, the law will always favor the copyright owner.

The use of a copyright owner's exclusive rights without permission or a "fair use" exception is considered an infringement. The law provides for very stiff penalties for infringing those rights because the use is inconsistent with the goal of encouraging the work of creative individuals.

Thus, before proceeding, you'll need to assess the level of risk that your organization can tolerate as well as how reasonably you've worked to obtain the necessary permission. A copyright holder may be more forgiving if you've documented your exhaustive efforts to obtain permission and have acknowledged their ownership of the material in your publication. The opposite is true if you've only made superficial, last minute attempts to obtain permission and have not included a statement of copyright acknowledgement.

Is there always a fee for using copyrighted material?

Because of the copyright owner's financial investment in developing the material, many copyright owners charge a fee for the right to reproduce the material. If the request is for a one-time or local use, the fee may be reduced or waived, but permission is still required. Many copyright owners will not grant a blanket permission to use copyrighted material and instead will require you to purchase a reprint license or to contact them before each use.

Who should I contact if I want to reproduce a magazine article?

Magazines and journals typically purchase one-time rights to publish an article in a single issue of the publication and thus the publisher can't grant permission for the material to be subsequently reproduced. Permission must be obtained directly from the author.

Are illustrations, photographs, and other graphics protected by copyright?

Visuals, like the text of a publication, are protected by copyright.

Who should I contact if I want to reproduce an excerpt from anthologies, songbooks, or other collection?

Collections contain works from many different sources. Typically the publisher of a collection obtains permission only to use those copyrighted materials in a particular publication and is not authorized to grant permission for their use elsewhere.

If I've already bought the book, can I make copies of the material in it?

The purchase of a book is just that—the purchase of physical copies. The right to make copies is one of the exclusive rights that always belong to the copyright holder and you will need to obtain permission before making copies. Although the fact that you own copies may influence the fee that the copyright holder charges to reproduce the material, it does not remove the obligation to obtain permission.

If I retype the copyrighted material, is it necessary to get permission to make copies?

It does not matter whether you photocopy it, calligraphy it on parchment, or chisel it in stone: if you are making additional copies of copyrighted work and what you're doing is not a "fair use" of the material, then you will need to get permission from the owner of the copyright. Regardless of what method you use to make the copies, the right to reproduce the material in any form is one of the exclusive rights owned by the copyright holder.

If a publication is out of stock, can I get permission to make copies?

If a publication is temporarily unavailable, the publisher will often grant permission to make as many copies as you have on order, provided the copies are destroyed once your order arrives.

Why should I pay a fee for the right to reproduce out-of-print material?

Out-of-print publications are often protected by copyright. (See above.) The fees charged for permission to reproduce out-of-print materials represent compensation to the copyright holder for use of only the copyrighted creative material in the publication and do not reflect the cost of manufacturing the publication. Thus, permission fees are usually far lower than the cost of purchasing the publication. The fees collected from permissions are typically shared with the creative contributors to the publication.

Is it necessary to obtain permission if I plan to adapt the material?

You must obtain permission to make changes in copyrighted material. Preparing new arrangements, abridgments, and other adapted versions derived from the original publication is considered the exclusive right of the copyright owner. The preparation of these derivative works requires the copyright owner's consent.

Is there a list of all the public domain works?

Although there are reference works that can help you research the status of a particular copyright, there is no definitive list of what is in the public domain. It would be nearly impossible to prepare and maintain a comprehensive list because materials can be considered public domain for many different reasons, including:

- The copyright term, including all available renewal periods, may have expired.
- The copyright was not renewed at the appropriate time.
- The copyright notice was omitted/improperly published according to the requirements of the copyright law in effect when it was published. Also, new translations of public domain texts or new musical arrangements of public domain tunes can appear to give new copyright protection to old, familiar works.

The copyright holder I'm looking for is no longer in business. Where do I go for permission?

Begin by contacting a local bookstore, music store, or the public library. All may be helpful in tracking the current owner of the copyright. An Internet search on the publisher's name may also provide information about the current owner or administrator of the copyrights.

How do I learn more about the copyright law?

For information about the United States copyright law, contact the U.S. Copyright Office at (202) 707-3000 or visit their helpful web site: www.lcweb.loc.gov/copyright/

Event Publications and the Use of Copyright Materials

If you're planning an event, you may wish to include preexisting material in your event publications. Obtaining permission is as easy as 1-2-3!

1.Determine the copyright status of the materials you wish to reproduce.

In addition to arranging the location, speakers, special music, and lighting and sound systems, select the material that you'd like to include in event publications. Early planning is essential to assure that you have sufficient time (four to six weeks) to obtain permission to use the copyrighted materials you'd like to reproduce.

As you select materials to reproduce for use at your event, determine if any or all of the material is protected by copyright or if it is in the public domain. If it's protected by copyright, you'll speed the permission process by locating the original source of the material and making a copy of the material to include with your request. If you don't have access to the original source, it's still helpful to include a copy of the material as you've found it used in another publication.

2. Contact the copyright administrator for permission to reprint material.

Be specific about what you want to reproduce and how you want to use it. (See sample letter.) Most publishers require your request in writing that is delivered by post, fax, or e-mail; a phone call may be sufficient if printing deadline are impending. Allow at least three weeks for a reply.

3. Include the copyright notice requested by the owner.

In response to your request, you'll receive a letter containing specific credit lines that must appear with the copyrighted material. Either a footnote or a notice in an acknowledgment section of the publication can be an appropriate place to cite the owner's copyright claim. Often a copyright owner will specify the location and require a copy to verify that you have printed the notice as they requested. No acknowledgment is necessary if a work is in the public domain.

Sample letter requesting permission

Date

Name
Address
City, State Zip

Dear (Name or Permissions Department):

I am writing to request permission to reprint the following:

Material to be copied: (name of the item as it appears in the original publication; include a copy when possible)

Composer/text author: (name)

Our source: (title and publisher)

Page number: (specify)

This material would be used as follows:

If for a publication, include: the name of the publication, the format (paper/cloth/electronic), number of pages, distribution (local, national), publisher, selling price (if any), number of copies

If for an event, include: the name of the sponsoring organization, event date, number of copies

May we have your permission to reprint this material? If you cannot grant permission for this use, I would appreciate any information you may be able to provide on the copyright holder.

For your convenience, a release form is provided below. Please specify the credit line, as well as any other conditions you may have for this use, and return a copy of this letter to me.

I thank you in advance for your prompt attention to this request. Please contact me as soon as possible if you have any questions. Thanks for your assistance.

Sincerely,

Name

Organization

(Address, if not printed on letterhead)

Telephone number (and FAX when applicable)

Email address

PERMISSION IS HEREBY GRANTED FOR THE USE DESCRIBED ABOVE.

Signature _____   Date _____   Fee _____

Copyright credit line _____

Chapter 16

What's Beyond:
The Communication Future

By Gary R. Rowe

What isn't going to change:

Religious institutions are primarily and fundamentally storytelling institutions. Stories of creation and the Creator, stories of prophecy, stories of eternal truths, stories of the engagement of the human and the divine, these will be, always, at the heart of faith communication.

What will change:

The future will be different not in the sense of what we do so much as how we go about doing it. We may have come a long way from circuit riders but we have a long way to go to catch up with the challenging opportunities of the digital world!

Metaphors are useful ways to advance the truths inherent in a good story. Imagine that this story of the future is served by a metaphor for an industrial age we have just left behind, the age of the machine, measured roughly from the invention of standard time to the first moon landing. We are now living in a new information age, the age of the electron, that is only beginning to emerge from the fog of accelerating change into something that we can see and that is beginning to shape our destinies.

Imagination and Dreaming

Imagine you are a youthful bystander at Kitty Hawk a hundred years ago. Can you imagine that you will, in your lifetime, cruise to Europe on a 747 in a matter of mere hours? Any communicator trying to discern the future while we stand here on the threshold of a new century—indeed, a new millennium—confronts a similar challenge to the imagination.

In 1998, an educational association assembled a "Council of 21" at Mount Vernon to imagine the features of schools and school systems America needs in the 21st century. Despite the presence of a well-known futurist, a former astronaut, media executives, government representatives, and leading educators, it was nearly impossible for the dialogue to achieve lift off and soar above the drudgery of contemporary school politics. The debates about curriculum standards and the grinding difficulties of achieving reform weighed down the imagination with the detritus of the past and present.

Is it any less difficult for our religious institutions to imagine the future? The age and history of our traditions can be a weight that keeps our thinking earthbound. But openness to new ways of thinking based on a careful inventory of the past and a creative understanding of the present are the keys to unlocking a useful vision of the future. Without these assessments and intuitions any group is likely to stagnate under the pressures of the moment.

While the council's deliberations about schools resulted in an important study that points the way toward a more vital future it was not as daring as it might be. Look back in time. Free, public education is a relatively new phenomenon. Why is that? If the human race got along for centuries without such schools, might we do so again? Not because humans will return en masse to a state of innocence or ignorance but because it is possible to organize learning without busses and buildings, textbooks and bell schedules. To ask the question of why we might need schools at all is to raise questions about fundamentals. In addressing these daring questions we might achieve some creative thinking that illuminates the otherwise imperceptible future.

Similar daring is required as religious communicators look to the future.

Such questions sound negative. They require us to use our imaginations to deconstruct that which currently exists. But answering these kinds of questions requires more than imagination. It requires dreaming. Dreaming is the imagination set free. It allows us to head for the exits of what is and enter a state of thinking about what might be. It is the formula for getting to levels of imaginative thought that hover above the ground of reality, without the supports of convention and precedent.

Think back to those who marveled at Gutenberg's moveable typography. Surely, many were fascinated by the mechanics. But did any onlookers anticipate the spread of literacy? More importantly, did anyone think to himself, "The monarchs of this world are in trouble"?

Electronic Space and Time

Children of the 1950s were the last generation to see giant steam locomotives speed heavy tonnage across the American landscape or wheel a fast express filled with people from city to town to city. The Iron Horse was an obvious machine. Watching it pass was to watch it in the act of work, side rods churning, stack belching smoke, steam hissing from its chambers, all noise and purpose.

Children today are the first humans to have the Internet since the day they were born. How does it work? Can anyone "see" it? Is it any less substantial if it's invisible?

There is more to be discerned from a nostalgic look to the past and an obvious fact about the present. One of the keys to dreaming about the future is to take a careful look at the trends in the recent past and in the present that are already working to alter our reality and ask, "Do these changes continue into the future and in what ways?" "What new things will these changes spawn that we haven't imagined?"

There is no question that industrial America has receded into the background of the economy, replaced by an information economy. The industrial age, the realm of the machine, had a kind of steadfast reality to it. Not only was it more or less obvious to understand work by seeing it, like the steam locomotive, this logic of labor enveloped workers in a spatial and temporal way of knowing the world by knowing the machine. Industries were located near natural resources; cities were efficient interchanges of everything from goods to capital. Religious beliefs were neatly organized into "denominations." Call this "M" space; the space and time of the mechanical world.

Religious adherents in M space lived in a social reality where time was neatly divided between work, home, leisure, and spiritual life. Life included conversation, family dinners and, in many cases, regular devotions. People lived in neighborhoods that were largely defined by actually knowing the neighbors. Spiritual questions might haunt the psyche but were quieted by conformity with one's own religious group. Voices that challenged convention were often perceived as the voices of misfits, iconoclasts, editorialists, or malcontents. (Of course, we are generalizing here.)

Then we slowly entered the untamed world of "E" space, where the physics of electrons, not giant locomotives, define the metaphors for space and time. Here is where a mechanistic world-view is disassembled. Cities lose their centers. Neighborhoods are real estate collectives. Office "parks" are magnets for soul grinding auto traffic. Domestic reality is infused and blended by continuous information and non-stop entertainment opportunities. Work is accomplished by tasks that are unseen, many hidden in telecommunications networks and across the vast bureaucracies of corporations.

The preceding paragraph describes, in part, the painful transition from M space to E space. We now only dimly perceive E space. It operates in a unfamiliar geography. In E space, what's more important to know, the address where a person lives, or the telephone number or e-mail address that connects to them? E space devalues physical location, among many other things.

In E space families have chaotic schedules. Work blends into leisure. Information is everywhere. Sorting is more important than receiving. We don't pay much attention to voices challenging authority. We look, sometimes in vain, for sources that have authority. What authority does the preacher, the priest, the religious leader have in this fast-paced, all-at-once social milieu?

The Mass Media Dissolution

The transition from M space to E space has happened in a span of roughly 50 years, a period indexed by the medium of television.

In the beginning we enjoyed broadcasting—at first, radio with pictures, but later a powerful influence on taste, manners, civic beliefs, and political passions. During the early years of broadcasting a few decision makers on 6th Avenue in New York City determined what the American public would see, aggregated in mass audiences.

Cable television defined the second stage of this infant medium. Specialized channels fragmented the traditional broadcast schedule into channels for all news, all weather, all movies, all comedy—anything a viewer could want and all the time!

The third stage of television was nearly simultaneous with the second: the arrival of the appliance-based channel. With VCRs, a viewer could shift program decision-making power from 6th Avenue to his or her own household. (The theatrical motion picture industry, also a medium in search of a mass audience, greeted the advent of VCRs with vulgarities and denials. Now distribution on tapes and discs form the largest revenue streams back to the studios).

The fourth stage in the evolution of television is now beginning. It has nothing to do with picture definition, aspect ratio or screen size. It has everything to do with personal sovereignty over content. Call it personal television. Whatever is on, what it connects to on the Web or elsewhere, the levels of interactivity with the information are all under the control of a new sovereign, the former couch potato.

The battle is on in the industry for control of the set-top box, the information portal, the hard drive that provides control for time shifting, program management and commercial skipping. Those engaged in this battle still fail to recognize that control will never be theirs again. It is as if the monarchies of programmers are dethroned by the restless peasants.

With the shift from analog to digital production, television has also evolved into a personal tool. Digital camcorders provide commercially acceptable images. Million dollar production suites now reside on personal computers for a few hundred dollars. Producing a television program is analogous to word processing with point-and-click, drag-and-drop simplicity. While these powerful tools don't make great producers any more than word processing makes great writers, the availability of these tools puts the means of production into the hands of what used to be the audience. (Watch the kids. See what they do with it).

This evolution of television marks a transition from the M space paradigm, mechanical industry, to the turbulent, newly democratic, and interconnected fabric of E space. It is not simply a new way to understand devices in the work place or household and how they work. It is a whole new way of understanding the world and managing life in it.

Standing On Our Knees

Several large communications companies paid a king's ransom for a market study in the early 1990s. With the explosive growth of personal computers and information appliances like fax machines, cellular telephones, laptops, and modems then underway, these companies wanted to make correct strategic decisions about the future of their businesses. The study was considered comprehensive and reliable because of a telephone survey of several thousand American households.

During the question-and-answer period that followed the confident presentation of the researchers in one of these companies the study crashed to earth on the basis of one question: "Did you talk to any children?" After all, children are not ignorant of these technologies, they're immersed in them.

To a child, a forecaster's question, "Do you have or want to have a cell phone?" would be utterly ridiculous. Contemporary children are not dazzled by the new technologies and devices that amaze their parents. They are born into a world where these things are ordinary. Children expect all of these things to be part, not just of what they do, but who they are.

According to current media studies, between connections at home and the ones at school, 99 percent of middle school children now have access to the Internet. A current study of the American household indicates that nearly half of all children either have or want to have a personal Web site.

The dexterity and knowledge of many youth have upset the traditional balance of parent or teacher and the child. Educational leaders cry for more money for professional development so teachers can acquire skills with technologies when the cheapest solution is to get teachers comfortable with the authority over technologies their children already bring to school. The kids know how to build the Web pages, run the computer simulations, and create the multimedia presentations.

It's time, perhaps, for adults to stop looking down and get down to look, eyeball-to-eyeball, with the children who know more about E space than they do.

The Reality of Appearance

A group of scholars, translators and media producers began work in 1991 on the possibility of translating a passage from the New Testament of the Bible in an audio-visual form. This was not to be an enactment of scriptures in the style of a Hollywood epic. Rather, it was to be the dynamic equivalent of a printed translation; but seen and heard, not read as text from a printed page. With the coming of technologies to interconnect a video signal with computer storage, it was to be supported by extensive study helps to illuminate the translation.

In blazing a promising path into the future, the team discovered something very old: they were, in a manner of speaking, re-inventing the Bible before its captivity by the Gutenberg technology. The Bible, after all, lived in memorization, vocalization, performance, song, and visual display long before it was printed. For some, this gave rise to new thinking about printed communications and relationships between tangible books and the less tangible forms of mediation accomplished electronically. Can it be that the transition to visually based communications that began with the photograph and continued in the motion picture and in television is a shift as profound as the one caused by Gutenberg? This may be one of the more challenging features of the emerging future to discern.

What the 20th century wrought in media is new, it marks irrevocable change, it's creating different habits of mind and human behavior. It is the first time one generation could pass on images and voices of itself, beyond death, to succeeding progeny. That shift is profound. It may be worth describing it in millennial terms. It will not dethrone print or books, but it will radically alter the variety of ways in which humans acquire information, communicate with others, and influence the world around them.

Our forebears thought of foreign mission fields as remote and alien because they were reached by sailing ships. We now live in a world where peasant farmers in India follow soybean prices at the Chicago Board of Trade on the Internet. What is "foreign" anymore? Who is our neighbor? Where are the mission fields of the present and future located?

Our New Sovereignty

A panel of five third graders sat in the well of an amphitheatre at Montana State University and spoke to a gathering of 80 school superintendents, a U.S. Senator and his staff, and their own teacher. They presented a digital video and a Web site they had created to commemorate the coming bicentennial of the Lewis and Clark expedition. One girl punctuated the presentation with her answer to an adult's question, "Well, the PowerPoint stuff is supposed to be for college kids but we used it."

The future is contained in this young girl's declaration. She is one of a new kind of storyteller. She heralds the expectations of our newest humans who are already acclimated to the opportunities of the digital world and to living life in E space. Their expectations are more daring than the defenders of what has been.

Traditional broadcasters seem to assume that their audience will always be there for them; all they have to do is create popular programs. As one network executive put it in the early 1980s, "Cable will never amount to anything." In a few short years he was working for a cable company. Subsequently, the traditional networks, to save their own franchises, bought up cable networks.

Recently, 12 percent of the coveted 18 to 34 male demographic disappeared from prime-time viewing measurements. The broadcast networks immediately faulted the ratings system as if people couldn't possibly find anything better to do with their time than watch television. But interactive games—as an online group activity—and the many temptations of the World Wide Web continue to erode traditional media habits.

Digital camcorders and digital editing on the desktop have little impact so far on media use. But what will happen in the near term and the long term? What used to be the passive audience may well become the active creators of new media. The camcorder is a new pencil; the editing software a new word processor that makes it easy to write with images and sounds.

Consider the experience of a church in Atlanta, Georgia. The stewardship committee determined to use media to present a case for increased pledges using PowerPoint slides loaded with statistics, budgets, and demographics. A producer challenged the group to sing a jingle for a brand of toothpaste that disappeared from store shelves many years ago. All laughed with the immediate recall of that silly music. Affectional memory is a powerful mnemonic device!

As ideas evolved into a short documentary video, committee members began to realize that many new members knew next to nothing about the history of the church, its commitment to stay in the city, its historic role in promoting child welfare in the depths of the depression, its open-doors meeting the challenges of racial integration, and its influence on the political culture of the city. Moreover, current members might read about the church's many programs for children, youth, social outreach and the like. But that doesn't mean they ever actually saw those programs in action. In brief, the creation of a video was an opportunity for an institution to learn new things about itself by a show-and-tell process.

So, for the little girl in Montana and the congregation in Atlanta the world has changed in a dramatic way. "Who gets to produce television (or media)?" Anyone.

Digital Intimacy

An extension of the question, "Who gets to make media?" is "Who gets to make meaning?" If it can be anyone, then the stories we tell in media may begin to feel much more personal and relevant. The traditional "audience" for media is meant to be dazzled by media but the personal "recipient" of media will feel a quite different response.

If the ability to tell powerful stories in media has moved from the towers of Sixth Avenue to the desktop of any child, then a dramatic shift in personal power is occurring in our society. How will this shift influence the work of faith communication in the future?

The disaggregation of mass media begs the question, "How big does an audience have to be to justify the production of a television program?" For the congregation in Atlanta, 800 members. For the third grader in Montana, a classroom of 25.

While broadcast networks will continue to attract large audiences for our more tribal rituals—the World Series, the Academy Awards, election night, and so forth—the time people spend with media is likely to shift dramatically in the direction of more intimate forms of information. Local cyber centers in some cities are experimenting with neighborhood originated programming over public access cable channels. Some faith communities are collecting oral histories from their members. Family reunions, high school games, civic ceremonies, local elections, all rank in importance for the smaller audiences of a town or city neighborhood and are undiminished sources of entertainment and information whether or not the production values approach those of traditional television.

Our children's capacity to be pioneering innovators in media is a forecast of how they will want to be reached as they grow into adults. What will a paper catalog do to influence purchases compared to an animated e-mail? Why would a person decide to watch a program on television unless it fits a profile of known personal interests? Why can't a meeting occur online instead of a physical place at the end of a long commute? Why can't my neighborhood in cyberspace be the forum for my block party?

Small businesses are already harnessing such media as DVDs for local advertising and promotion with far greater impact than tradition print and direct mail. Digital media are proving to be a tool for economic development and professional training. Pressure on the tuition fees for continuing education will face the pressures of desktop-produced, cheaply distributed media. Faith communities need to take note of these dynamics.

In all these examples, and many more that could be cited, it is not only the content of the messages that create a sense of intimacy. The ways in which such messages are marketed will give them high value on personal agendas. A religious assembly might have a central location but the members may also constitute a virtual network that ties them together in between worship gatherings. Affinity organizations might spring up around a neighborhood clean-up campaign or a broader social agenda such as a prison ministry. Preparation for religious education might occur online or on the family's DVD player. Messages, in short, that feel personal and relevant will find and reach a recipient!

Making Meaning in Media

Once upon a time, the opportunity to communicate in multiple media, including television, would have been available only at great expense and would have required a substantial staff and balky equipment. Those days, fortunately, are gone. It is now possible for a faith community to create powerful content and tools in all forms of digital media. The book you hold in your hands was created with no typewriters and no moveable type. In fact, it didn't need to be anything but digital information until it rolled on the printing press. This represents merely a primitive beginning for the power that comes with an integrated, comprehensive plan to use media.

In order to harness the power of digital media you need only a computer on a desktop, a camera or camcorder, and not much more. Think of this as a "digital workbench" for the writer, the designer, and the editor. But it's more than that.

Digital media have democratized information. There is no need to limit content to what is created by acknowledged professionals. Just as the Kodak camera blurred the lines between professional photographers and amateurs, there's no reason to not include the submissions of members from all walks of life and from children in the things you produce on your workbench.

Digital media provide opportunities to exchange information. Submissions from far-flung places gathered electronically can end up in an institutional magazine or on a Web site or in a video.

Digital media can help create community. There is dynamic at work much like the fascination of "seeing myself on TV" that can animate digital media to make it feel personal. Communities can form at institutional or neighborhood levels or both, with one supporting the content of the other.

Digital media establish a forum for collaboration. A work in progress doesn't have to be a work that gets finished. The "call and response" afforded by digital information pathways means people can build content together.

Digital media create a new form of publishing house. The traditional definitions of writing and editing from the print world will fall before the many creative collaborators involved in digital media. What is meant by publishing will be transformed by the myriad opportunities to distribute information anywhere in the world with minimal costs. The publishing house is transformed by a new model: the information studio.

 ## Bringing the Future Nearer

Judging success at harnessing these opportunities in our faith communities is not easily ascertained at this early stage of the journey into E space. But there are a number of useful things to think about that may help assure success.

Are you marketing your message? In a world increasingly saturated by information, it's necessary to let the right people know your message is available. Religious organizations need to work as communications networks linked in as many ways as possible to constituents.

Are you finding your audience? Is there sufficient feedback and solicitations for more information to indicate that people care about the messages transmitted?

Are your messages available every day, all the time, anywhere? There's no reason for them not to be.

Are you forming relationships? New forms of interactive software can run on computer desktops and send alerts about the availability of new information or as a reminder of a daily devotion or a host of other uses. People who accept such software devices are effectively joining your network.

Are you representing your "audience"—readers, viewers, listeners? Do your new messages include the feedback you received from previous messages? Are new stories discovered because of the way you told a previous story and is this obvious (because you show that you care)?

Do you encourage others to imitate your work? If you are communicating at the denominational level, encourage local congregants to adopt what they wish of your formats, editorial designs, and graphics. And grant permission to share content. Digital media make it easy to discard outmoded notions of "my" copyright versus "your" use or it should, at least, in faith communications.

In how many media are you working? Be prepared to serve as many "audiences" as possible in any medium they choose. This will help to cross-promote multiple ways to circulate information and reach a wider constituency.

Remember all the talk about the 500 channel world that swept the television industry in the 1990s? Many scoffed at the thought. There's a company already in business with its floor space filled with terabyte servers. The company is capturing clients' feeds from satellite and cable, converting the signals in real time at 2MB-per-second rates and streaming them out onto the Web as full screen television. Many of their clients are religious institutions, mostly evangelical ministries. To watch the lights flashing on those servers is to see what may be the beginning of the 5-million-channel world. Kitty Hawk, indeed!

Are your messages good stories? As a wise person famously said, "The music is not in the piano." The importance of communications in faith communities is not in the technology but in the stories told. It is the ways these stories are produced and delivered that is about to change.

The formation of our faiths happened around the campfires of an earlier time, among people whose tents were pitched under the starlight of an ancient world. They were good stories then. That's why they are still with us. Blinking stars or blinking lights on servers, it is still our obligation to tell the stories of faith with all the creative means available to us.

Welcome to the future!

Authors

M. Garlinda Burton of Nashville, Tenn., was on the staff of United Methodist Communications from 1983-2003, most recently as editor of *INTERPRETER* magazine and director of the agency's Information Team. She is currently executive of the United Methodist Commission on the Status and Role of Women. She is also communications chairperson at Hobson United Methodist Church. Burton earned a bachelor's degree in journalism from the University of Tennessee at Knoxville and a master's degree from the Medill School of Journalism at Northwestern University in Evanston, Ill. GBurton@bellsouth.net

J. Ron Byler is associate executive director of Mennonite Church USA, a denomination of about 1,000 congregations. He has served as media relations director for American Friends Service Committee, associate director of Mennonite Media and a denominational executive for the Mennonite Church. As vice president for Genesis Communications, he was a consultant for many non-profit faith-based organizations. He is a video producer by training and he is a former executive director and board member of the Religion Communicators Council. rbyler@juno.com

Anuttama Dasa is director of communications and governing body commissioner for the International Society for Krishna Consciousness (ISKCON), a Vaishnava, or monotheistic, faith within Hindu culture. Dasa has been a member of the Religion Communicators Council since 1993, and has served as board member and national vice president. He also serves on the boards of the National Conference for Community and Justice in the Washington, D.C. region, and the Society for Hindu-Christian Studies of the American Academy of Religion. He is a convener of the annual Vaishnava-Christian dialogue, cosponsored by the U.S. Conference of Catholic Bishops. He and his wife, Rukmini, live in Maryland. anuttama.acbsp@pamho.net

Nancy Fisher is Senior Vice President/Director of Communications and member of the Executive Committee at the Church Pension Group in New York City. Responsibilities include strategic planning, advertising, graphic design, publications (newsletters, brochures, inserts, calendars, the annual report), videos, and press relations. Before joining CPG in 2000, she was an award-winning creator/producer/director of television programming and home videos, including two national cable TV series for Campbell Soup Company. nfisher@cpg.org

Daniel R. Gangler directs the communication ministries of the Indiana Area of The United Methodist Church and edits its publications in Indianapolis. A 25-year veteran of religion communication, prior to coming to his present position he was director of communications at the Christian Church (Disciples of Christ) Church Finance Council; managing editor of *The Disciple* magazine; associate editor of the Dallas-based *United Methodist Reporter* and online Reporter Interactive; and director of communications of the Nebraska Conference of The United Methodist Church in Lincoln. He serves as an ordained elder in The United Methodist Church. DGangler@inareaumc.org

Bret D. Haines is a graphic designer in Nashville, Tennessee. He has a MA in advertising design and a BS in graphic design, and also teaches graphic design at Watkins College of Art and Design in Nashville. Haines worked as art director for 17 years at the General Board of Higher Education and Ministry of The United Methodist Church. He produced award-winning publications, newsletters, logos, and Web sites. Haines currently runs BaaHaus Design in Nashville with his wife, Leslie. bret@BaaHaus.com

Kami S. Lund is a communications specialist for the Board of Pensions of the Evangelical Lutheran Church in America. She is responsible for writing, editing, and designing the Board of Pensions' newsletters and other communication materials. A main focus of her work is putting a "human face" on health, retirement and other benefits. Lund received a bachelor's degree in journalism from the University of Wisconsin at River Falls. She is a member of the International Association of Business Communicators, as well as the Religion Communicators Council. klund@elcabop.org

Jeanean D. Merkel is principal of Illumicon, a communications consultancy. She was until recently vice president of Paulist Media Works. She is a past president of RCC and also serves as vice president of the Catholic Academy for Communication Arts Professionals. She has extensive experience in assisting religious organizations to communicate their mission via print, radio, video, and web. She has edited many publications, including the book, *Creating a Home: Benchmarks for Church Leadership Roles for Women*. She holds a master's degree in religious studies from Georgetown University and a BA from Alverno College. jmerkel@illumicom.org

Kermit Netteburg is assistant to the president for communication for the Seventh-day Adventist Church in North America. In that capacity, he serves as president of the Adventist Media Center in Simi Valley, California. He leads two of the church's media ministries, serving as president of LifeTalk Radio, a network of more than 25 radio stations; and general manager of Adventist Communication Network, the church's internal television network with more than 1,500 downlink sites. He has worked in radio and television as executive producer, producer, director, consultant––and, on rare occasions, talent. Kermit.Netteburg@NAD.Adventist.org

Kimberly Pace, a preacher's kid from Mississippi, began her ministry as executive director of The United Methodist Hour and "on-air talent" for the radio and television program, Time that Makes the Difference. She is a graduate of Millsaps College, B.A., and Shenandoah University, M.M. Pace has served as a resource consultant with the Communications Resourcing Team at United Methodist Communications. In 2002, she joined the General Board of Discipleship of The United Methodist Church as the chief communications officer. She is a member of the United Methodist Association of Communicators, Religion Communicators Council, and West End UMC. In 2003 she was elected the Nashville Chapter President of Religion Communicators Council. KPace@GBOD.org

Rose Pacatte, MEd in Media Studies, is a member of the Daughters of St. Paul, a Roman Catholic community of women religious that use the media to promote the Word of God in today's culture. Sister Pacatte is the director of the Pauline Center for Media Studies in Los Angeles (Culver City), Calif., and is the co-author of the award-winning movie lectionary series, *Lights, Camera...Faith: A Movie Lover's Guide to the Scriptures* (Pauline Books & Media, Boston.) She writes the monthly "Eye on Entertainment" column for *St. Anthony Messenger* magazine and is an international presenter on media literacy education and spirituality and media. She is also co-founder of the National Film Retreat. rosepacatt@aol.com

Brad Pokorny is editor of *One Country*, the award winning public information periodical for the Bahá'í International Community. Published in seven languages, the newsletter reaches more than 50,000 people in 180 countries. Before coming to the Bahá'í International Community in 1987, Brad was a staff reporter at *The Boston Globe*. He has an undergraduate degree from The Evergreen State College in Olympia, Washington, and a graduate degree in government from Harvard University in Cambridge, Mass. He lives in New Hampshire with his wife and children. bpokorny@bic.org

Rachel Riensche is attorney for Minnesota Public Radio and was vice president for Corporate Affairs at Augsburg Fortress, the Publishing House of the Evangelical Lutheran Church in America. She has served in a variety of editorial, copyright, and legal positions, responsible for legal services, intellectual property management, archives/reference collections, and publishing services provided to ELCA churchwide units. A graduate of Wartburg College, Waverly, Iowa and William Mitchell College of Law, St. Paul, Minn., Riensche is a frequent speaker on copyright issues to church, college, and civic groups. RRiensche@aol.com

Gary R. Rowe heads a television and multimedia production company offering consulting and communications development services to clients in television, publishing, and new media. Clients include the American Bible Society, Atlanta History Center, National Public Radio, PBS, and many others. Previously, Rowe served as senior vice president of Turner Educational Services, a unit of Turner Broadcasting System, where he developed CNN NEWSROOM, an international program for schools, and Turner Adventure Learning, a series of interactive programs. Rowe was director of communications of the Church Federation of Greater Chicago, 1974-1981. GRowe@Rowemedia.com

The **Rev. Jay Sidebotham** has served as Vicar of St. Bartholomew's Episcopal Church in New York City since January 1999. He attended Trinity College in Hartford,CT and after graduation went to work in Manhattan, first at an animation studio working on Schoolhouse Rock educational cartoons, then in various ad agencies, until he made a 'slight career shift' to the ordination track. After studying at Union Theological Seminary in New York, he served at St. Martin's Church, in Providence, RI; St. Columba's, Washington DC; and as Rector of St. Luke's Church, Durham, NC. Sidebotham@stbarts.org

Bill Southern serves as the Director of Communication for the nearly 5000-member Richland Hills Church of Christ, a non-denominational Christian community in a northeast suburb of Ft. Worth, Texas. Southern joined the church staff in 1999 after a extensive career that included experience in printing, public relations, communications and financial consulting. He also brought to his current position 16 years of volunteer service in the sound, lighting, media, and communication ministries of the church. He is primary media contact for the church and oversees its Web site. An alumnus of Abilene Christian University and the University of Colorado, Southern also holds two degrees from the American College. Bill.Southern@rhchurch.org

Linda J. Svensk is publications manager for the Board of Pensions of the Evangelical Lutheran Church in America. She has worked at the Board of Pensions for 17 years, including two years with the predecessor Board of Pensions of the American Lutheran Church. She is responsible for planning and implementing the strategic objectives of the publications department and overseeing the development, production and printing of plan materials. She received a bachelor's degree in education from Augsburg College in Minneapolis. She is a member of The Association for Women in Communications, as well as the Religion Communicators Council. lsvensk@elcabop.org

Donn James Tilson is Associate Professor Advertising and Public Relations, University of Miami School of Communication. Dr. Tilson holds a Ph.D. from Stirling University in Scotland. He is an accredited member of the Public Relations Society of America (PRSA). He has served as a public relations manager for BellSouth and as past president and national assembly delegate of the Miami chapter of PRSA. He currently is national chair-elect of PRSA's International Division. DonnTilson@aol.com